Starting Out in Local History

Simon Fowler

COUNTRYSIDE BOOKS
NEWBURY, BERKSHIRE

COUNTRYSIDE BOOKS
3 Catherine Road
Newbury, Berkshire

To view our complete range of books,
please visit us at
www.countrysidebooks.co.uk

ISBN 1 85306 686 9

Cover design by KDP, Kingsclere

Produced through MRM Associates Ltd, Reading
Printed by Woolnough Bookbinding Ltd., Irthlingborough

CONTENTS

•••••

- Using written sources
- Making use of your research

INTRODUCTION

•••••

Local history is sometimes regarded as the poor relation to genealogy or family history. Why should we be interested in places and societies of the past, when there are our own ancestors, each with a unique story to tell, to discover? Yet, local history can be equally absorbing, and you don't have to worry about remembering who was related to whom.

Unlike genealogy, local history is what you make it. The subject is a broad canvas on which you make your own mark. You may just want to know why your street has a peculiar name, or be intrigued by a disused mill or railway building a few streets away from your home, or perhaps are keen to find out more about a local trade or industry. You can even study areas two or three hundred miles from where you live. What you do and how you do it is up to you. But beware – local history is addictive. Before you know it a simple query about the history of your house can turn into a life-long interest in tiles and tile makers.

In particular readers are urged, in the words of the greatest of all local historians, W.G. Hoskins, to go out and get mud on their boots, that is to explore the physical townscape and landscape to see what buildings and hedgerows can tell us about the past. This is a very different approach to most other books on the subject, which assumes that local historians are happier in the warmth of a library or archive.

Local history has often been its own worst enemy. Too many books – even those designated for the beginner – assume that you have a grasp of Latin, or spend pages telling you about medieval field patterns. This book is different. It assumes no prior knowledge on the part of the reader, just the desire to find out more about the locality in which they live and the forces which have shaped it.

We are lucky because so much remains to explore – whether on the ground in the form of old buildings and medieval street patterns, or held in archives in documents going back nearly a thousand years. Britain has not suffered the destruction of war to the same extent, as has been the case in many other countries. Many historic buildings have of course been lost over the centuries, but so much remains. Archival holdings too have not remained immune to the ravages of time, but even so record offices are over-flowing with historic material, much of it hardly touched since it arrived. They are all there for you to use. And it needn't cost much. Very few archives charge for admission and, of course, the streets are free to wander as you please. Archives and local studies libraries often have highly trained staff who are only too happy to point you in the right direction.

Like the famous sporting cliché, this book is a game of two halves. The first part consists of a series of short introductory essays on aspects of local history research, which I hope are both informative and encouraging. The second half is really a local history dictionary with more information about common records you may need to use, the places you might need to visit in the course of your research, and a glossary of some common terms you might come across. Where appropriate details of books and web sites are also included, so you can discover more if the need arises. Where something is explained in more detail in part two it is highlighted in **bold** in the text.

What more can I say, but ENJOY! Local history is an absorbing study, which if you are not careful, can take over your life. However deeply you become involved, don't forget it is meant to be fun.

I am grateful for the encouragement and support of Robert and Susan Howard of *Local History Magazine* (make their day, why not subscribe, see page 107!) and Nicholas Battle, Margaret Ward and Paula Leigh of Countryside Books in writing this book. Errors and omissions are of course my own.

Simon Fowler

1
DISCOVERING HISTORY WITH OUR EYES

●●●●●

Case History: Bishops Stortford

One of the great attractions of local history is that you can discover so much from just keeping your eyes peeled. Britain's greatest local historian, W.G. Hoskins once urged local historians to leave their warm archives and libraries to tramp the streets.

This chapter concentrates very much on what most of us might see while walking to the shops. You may protest that you do not live anywhere of any great antiquity. But even the most modern housing estates may have something of interest; perhaps an old farm building survives, or houses with distinctive architectural features, or the street names are based on the field names that once were there.

The pictures in this chapter were taken on a wintry morning in January 2001. Although I had grown up in Bishops Stortford, on the Hertfordshire/Essex border, it had been many years since I explored the town, and these photographs are of some of the things I came across during my walk from the station to my parents' house at the north end of the town. They merely scratch the surface, of course. Bishops Stortford grew up around a ford across the local river Stort and in Roman times Stane Street crossed the river here. It received its name from the Bishops of London, who built Waytemore castle in the town, and for centuries it was an important market place for wheat and barley. Canal, road and railway links have all made their mark, and today Stansted Airport makes its presence felt. There are many clues to this flow of history to be found, and no doubt locals would point out other interesting sights, but these photographs help to demonstrate that even very ordinary towns and buildings have something of note to local historians lying just beneath the surface.

GETTING STARTED

The first step is to get out of your chair and explore your local area. It isn't difficult. All you need is a jacket and a pair of shoes. You can't do this sort of thing by car, so leave it at home. You might also want to take:

- A street map. This can help explain certain features on the ground, though on the other hand do not become too constrained by the map, the whole point is to go where the fancy takes you. A current A-Z or equivalent map will do. Even better however would be to buy a reproduction of an old large scale Ordnance Survey **map** if one exists for your area so you can compare what a place looks like now with what it looked like a hundred or so years ago. These are often sold by local libraries and archives.
- A guidebook can sometimes be useful in giving background information on a building or street, but there is the temptation just to look at buildings described in it and ignore the rest. An alternative may be a town trail map produced by the local council or amenity society.
- A camera to take pictures of buildings and street scenes. A spare film might also come in handy.
- A small notebook, that can easily be slipped into a pocket, in which to jot down locations of the photographs you have taken, a description of the discoveries you have made, or questions that come to mind during the course of the walk.
- Have a destination in mind, such as a pub or tearoom, for a little light refreshment and a chance to reflect on what you've seen.

Two words of warning:

- Be very careful of traffic. It is very easy when you are engrossed in studying a building to step into the path of an oncoming car or bicycle.
- Don't try to do too much at once. A walk of this kind can be surprisingly tiring. It is better to do it in gentle stages and enjoy what you are finding.

Don't just stick to the main roads: interesting buildings and street scenes can often be found in side streets away from the town's centre.

Since the maltings at Bishops Stortford closed in the 1960s the buildings have been taken over by a variety of night clubs, restaurants and small businesses. The size of the maltings reflects the importance of the trade to the local economy.

King's Cottages were almshouses for the elderly built by Sir Walter Gilbey, the distiller, in memory of his wife. Alms houses are often some of the most architecturally interesting buildings to be found in a town. You may well find a plaque commemorating their founder.

You might be interested in recording the present urban landscape so that future generations can have some understanding of what the area was like. It is particularly important to record the inside of buildings, such as offices or pubs or people's homes. If this appeals to you, check with the local studies library to see whether a project of this kind is already underway. A good guide is Valerie Norrington, *Recording the Present* (British Association for Local History, 1989).

QUESTIONS, QUESTIONS

During your walk you should be trying to answer some, at least, of the following questions:

- What are the natural physical features (say, a river or a hill) in the neighbourhood?
- How have these features affected the development of the area you are looking at?
- What evidence is there of the area's social history, such as almshouses, war memorials and chapels?
- What does the evidence tell you about the area's economic history, such as markets, coaching inns, and other old buildings?
- What does the evidence tell you about the area's industrial history, such as canal-side wharves and railway viaducts, old mills or factories, docks and breweries?
- What can the types of housing (council estates, terraces, or detached houses) tell you about the development of the area?
- What can the parish church tell you about the history of the area? Was it medieval, endowed by wealthy wool merchants, or built in the 19th century to cater for an industrial population? What do the tombs and gravestones outside, and the monuments inside indicate about the people who worshipped there?

WHAT TO LOOK OUT FOR

STREETS

- Street furniture can easily be overlooked but can offer valuable clues on an area's history. Look out for examples of mile posts, parish boundary markers set into walls, drinking fountains and troughs for horses, statues and memorials, and plaques on the sides of buildings.

11

Tucked away in the side streets is the Old Police Station of 1890. Now used by several local and central government agencies: official buildings are often ignored but can be interesting in their own right.

Almost next door are two cottages from the 1820s. They are a curious survival in a street of offices, small shops and restaurants. Perhaps their owners refused to sell up when the area was being redeveloped in the 1880s and 1890s.

- Are there any unusual buildings in the street? Can you suggest a reason why they might be there?
- What sort of buildings line the street? What do they tell you about the people who lived or worked here? What social class do you think the original residents were?
- What signs are there of the street's changing fortunes over time – have the houses become gentrified or the factories derelict? Is there any evidence on the ground to support your theory?
- What economic activity took (or takes) place in the street? There may be factories, shops, even a pub. Is there any evidence to indicate why these activities take place here – is the street close to transport links or near the market?
- Are the buildings roughly of the same age? You may find on long streets, particularly main roads, that the further out you go the more recent the buildings. However, look out for a scattering of older buildings, perhaps a terrace of houses or an older detached house, amongst the more modern. Can you suggest reasons why this has occurred?
- Using an old map you might want to track the original route of a street. Many roads have been widened, straightened or even moved, over the centuries. There may be evidence of this on the ground, even if it is just a street name. You might consider why and when this occurred.

INDIVIDUAL BUILDINGS

These are various suggestions about looking at buildings:

- What at first glance do you think the building was designed for?
- When do you think it was built? A clue can sometimes be found on buildings designed for public use where there may be a foundation stone which says when the building was begun or completed.
- What is it built out of? In most cases the answer will be brick, but older buildings might be mainly wooden, and newer ones from concrete.
- Look at the floors above the ground floor. Even if the ground floor of a shop has been altered, quite often the first floor and above remain substantially as the architect intended.
- If a building has changed its use this may result in an odd appearance. It may be slightly out of proportion to its neighbours, or doors or windows may not be in the right place. And the house name may reflect former usage ('The Old Mill').

The small local market wraps itself around the Corn Exchange. The market is rather smaller than I remembered. Despite the rise in the town's population traders may well have suffered from the arrival of a number of supermarkets on the outskirts of town.

This short little alley may well have marked the original boundary of the market, but the incursion of the building to the left and the Corn Exchange reduced the space available.

- Without trespassing, try to look behind the building. Even if the front has been modernised by the Victorians or later generations, the back may remain substantially unaltered. You may be able to see extensions added or alterations made over the centuries. Out-houses, such as stables, coach houses or dovecots may provide further clues as to previous usage.

FURTHER READING

Mark Girouard, *The English Town* (Yale UP, 1990) traces the history of towns and many of the buildings you may find in any English urban area. It is also beautifully illustrated. Alec Clifton Taylor's *Six English Towns*, *Six More English Towns* and *Another Six English Towns* (BBC, 1977-1984) written to accompany the TV series of the same title are detailed accounts of a number of towns of interest. Another interesting book is Mick Aston and James Bond, *The Landscape of Towns* (Sutton, 2000), which despite the name is largely about the growth of urban areas. Although Michael Stratton and Barrie Trinder, *Industrial England* (Batsford, 1997) is largely an introduction to **industrial archaeology**, there are useful sections about the architecture of factories, mills and railways.

To follow up, in archives and local studies libraries, questions which have arisen out of your walk Stephen Potter, *Exploring Urban History: Sources for Local Historians* (Batsford, 1990) is a good introduction. Slightly more dated is David Stenhouse, *Understanding Towns* (Wayland, 1977). A useful guide to the records is John West, *Town Records* (Phillimore, 1983). Primarily of interest to teachers, although it is an excellent guide to source material and research topics is Frank Grace, *The Late Victorian Town* (British Association for Local History, 1991).

A number of books look at the rural landscape, notably W.G. Hoskins' *Making of the English Landscape* (Penguin Books, 1970) and *Fieldwork in Local History* (Faber, 1982), Richard Muir's *The New Guide to Reading the Landscape: Fieldwork in Local History* (Exeter University Press, 2000), Maurice Beresford, *History on the Ground* (Sutton, 1998) and Trevor Yorke, *Tracing the History of Villages* (Countryside Books, 2001).

Architecturally perhaps the finest of the town's pubs, the Black Lion now masquerades as 'Scruffy Macs'. This 16th century tavern surely deserves a better fate than becoming an Irish theme pub.

The Boar's Head is another attractive inn: one that fortunately seems to have escaped the more outrageous schemes of the brewers. Situated opposite the church it appears almost to have started life as a merchant's house.

LOOKING AT STREET NAMES

The origin of street names can make an interesting study. Some local history societies may have published guides, so check at the library to see whether they can help. Remember that:

- Streets can change their names for various reasons or for no apparent reason at all.
- The original name may be corrupted over the centuries – or have been amended by the Victorians for reasons of taste or antiquity, thus Piss Passage may have been renamed Puss or Pitt.
- They may have an official name but be called something else by residents.

Trade and street **directories** will give a rough idea when streets were built and whether there were name changes at any time. Large-scale **maps** are perhaps less useful, as they were not published annually. The decision to name roads can usually be found in the minutes of local councils and their predecessors. Checking the names of the oldest roads in the centre of town may necessitate studying Tudor and Stuart records or even go back to the medieval period.

Street names generally fall into the following five categories:

- Those which refer to an activity which took place in the area, such as Market Street or Ship Street (where sheep may have been kept before they were sold).
- Describes what might be found (or have been found) on the street, such as Station Road or Harbour Street. St Michael's Street might take you to St Michael's church. They may also describe features which are no longer there, such as farms or fields and physical features such as hills (Hill Street) or rivers (Water Lane).
- Describes the direction, North Street normally goes north, and London Road usually signifies that this is the road to take to get to London.
- Be named after people or an historical event. The individuals can be national figures or former local dignitaries. Events however tend to be the better known celebrations or British triumphs.
- Reflect the whim (or lack of imagination) of the developer, which is why you may find a succession of streets named after poets, towns or even his children. Street names may also be a part of an attempt to make a development seem more attractive than perhaps it really is.

The finest street in the town is undoubtedly the wide Windhill, which leads from the parish church of St Michael to the local public school, Bishops Stortford College. Census returns might confirm my suspicion that middle-class families have always occupied the houses here.

This 18th century cottage spent most of its life as a public house – 'the Fox', although the casual observer might never guess. Local people, especially elderly residents, can give you information about buildings and their uses which it might be difficult to find elsewhere. One slight clue as to the cottage's former use is the coy street name 'Reynard Copse' given to a cul-de-sac of houses which occupy what used to be the pub garden.

2
GETTING STARTED IN LOCAL HISTORY

•••••

When you first become interested in a subject it is natural to want to find out what has already been written about it. Some topics, especially railway and transport, are well served by **secondary material**, that is books and periodicals.

The easiest thing to do is to talk to the local studies librarian at your county library. Most central, or other large, libraries have a local studies section, which, as the name suggests, keeps books and other material on the locality. Local studies librarians can be very helpful. They should be able to tell you if any books or articles have been written on your subject. If they do not have the book you want they should be able to order it on inter-library loan, which might cost a few pounds but could save many wasted hours of research.

In places where there is no local studies library, you might try the local museum, which may well have a small library and archive collection. The curator will often be able to answer your questions or point you towards books and other sources which could help with further research.

If you have access to the internet there may well be a website for your area or about your topic to help you get started, although you should always treat the content with caution as many sites contain errors.

FAMILY HISTORY AND LOCAL HISTORY

Don't forget that local historians can use genealogical resources with advantage. Many books and booklets published by family history societies (especially the Federation of Family History Societies) offer very useful advice. The Gibson Guides, edited by Jeremy Gibson for the Federation, are particularly valuable. A free catalogue of current publications can be obtained from the FFHS (Publications) Ltd, Units 115–16 Cheatham Industrial Estate, Oram St, Bury BL9 6EN.

You can browse through books and other items sold by family history societies and other suppliers at family history fairs. The largest one is organised by the **Society of Genealogists** and normally takes place over the first weekend of May in London, but almost every town now has an annual event. A comprehensive list is published in *Family History Monthly* every January.

BOOKS

There are several series of books which can provide very useful introductions to the histories of a county, town or village. Unless otherwise indicated these books should be available in local studies libraries, county record offices or university libraries.

COUNTY SURVEYS

1. *Victoria County Histories*

For many counties there is a series of Victoria County History volumes (VCH). The Victoria History of the Counties of England was started in 1899 with the aim of providing the definitive history of each English county. The original intention was to complete the project within a few years, but a century or so later the work is still continuing. Each county history consists of a series of volumes containing both 'general' and 'topographic' chapters. The general chapters cover subjects such as pre-history, and ecclesiastical and economic history for the whole county. The topographical chapters give a comprehensive account of each city, town and village in the county.

The VCH is especially strong on buildings and the medieval and early-modern (ie the Tudor and Stuart) period. The early volumes, particularly those completed before the First World War, are certainly not as comprehensive or rigorous as the more modern work, but have a period charm of their own. Appendix IV lists publications by county. Over the next few years it is hoped that part of the Histories will be made available on the internet. For more about this development, visit the VCH's web site (*www.englandpast.net*).

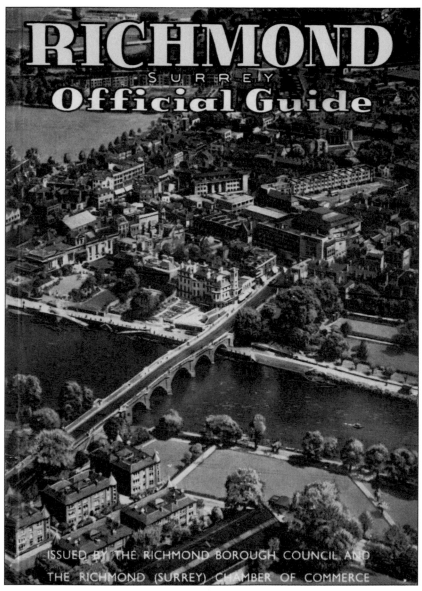

RICHMOND
SURREY
Official Guide

Many places published, and indeed still publish, official guides to promote local industries and shops, as well as tourist attractions. As a result these guides can provide an initial, if always optimistic, survey of a town and its economy. This guide for Richmond was published in the mid-1950s.

21

2. *The Buildings of England*

If you are interested in particular buildings, you will often find a short description in the relevant volume of *The Buildings of England*. Over a thirty-year period, Sir Nikolaus Pevsner prepared a detailed architectural guide to the counties of England. Prominent or interesting buildings in each town and village are briefly described, often with a comment on their architectural merit. Volumes also contain a useful introductory essay to architectural developments in the area. Pevsner completed his work in 1974, although volumes have subsequently been updated.

3. *County histories*

During the 19th century (and earlier) a number of amateur historians attempted to write the histories of their counties, with varying degrees of success. Although most of the scholarship in these histories has long been superseded, they occasionally prove to be of use. These books are often to be found at local studies and university libraries. They are described in more detail in C.R.J. Currie and C.P. Lewis, *A Guide to English County Histories* (Sutton Publishing, 1994).

4. *Other series*

On sale in almost every town and larger villages are books of old photographs or local stories about the area. Some are produced by publishers such as Countryside, Phillimore, Sutton or Breedon, while others are published by local history societies. The quality of the photographs and the accompanying captions can vary, but, even so, they offer an interesting introduction to the locality's history.

During the 1960s and 1970s the publisher Robert Hale produced the *Portrait of Britain* series of books, which were accounts of counties or other areas of particular interest. These books are readily available in libraries, and although by no means academic still offer a good introduction to local districts.

Before the Second World War, Arthur Mee wrote many county histories in his *King's England* series. The books are arranged by place, often with atmospheric photographs. He took a now rather dated anecdotal approach, but even so they offer a fascinating portrait of a world that has largely disappeared. Although a few volumes were reprinted a few years ago, the series in general is long out of publication. The best place to find these books is in second-hand bookshops.

Another publisher, Batsford, before the Second World War, produced a *Portrait of Britain* series which is also worth looking out for in second-hand bookshops. Largely as a result of their attractive Art Deco dust-jackets, these are very collectable so can be expensive.

OTHER PUBLICATIONS

Many counties have a county record society which exists to publish transcripts of old documents, so it is possible that there may already be some original records about your locality in print. The local studies library should have these books. If you have difficulty finding a particular volume the **Public Record Office** (PRO) Library has an almost complete set for the whole country. Many are also held at the **Society of Genealogists** (SoG). Most towns have a local history society which usually publishes a journal or pamphlets on aspects of local history. Again, copies of these publications are often found at local study libraries.

Curiously, guidebooks can also offer an interesting perspective on a town or local attractions, although they are more likely to exist for places that attracted tourists. The first guidebooks date from the late 18th century, but come into their own by the middle of the 19th century when the railways made cheap and speedy travel available to millions of people.

Over the centuries writers have toured England and reported about their experiences, which can give an interesting perspective for local historians. The first such account was John Leland's *Itinerary* which he presented to Henry VIII in 1546. Other famous travels are those undertaken by Daniel Defoe between 1724 and 1726 in *A Tour Through the Whole Island of Great Britain*, William Cobbett's *Rural Rides*, which mainly took place in Southern England during the 1820s, and J.B. Priestley's *English Journey* published in 1934. If you are interested in the 17th century, John Aubrey's *Brief Lives* is a fascinating account of the personalities and the gossip of the period. All these books are readily available in libraries and in paperback editions. There are many other diaries and accounts which might be of use in your researches: the local studies librarian should be able to direct you to interesting ones for the area you are studying.

II.—Exeter as a Travel-centre and Mid-Devon.

ITS central position as regards sea, river, railway and moorland makes Exeter one of those places in which holiday-makers of all classes delight to tarry. As the capital of a county should do, the chief-town of Devonshire commands still, as it did in far-off Roman times, the highways to all that is important and interesting either in the interior of the "Shire of the Sea Kings," or on its northern and southern shores. The country immediately surrounding Exeter is typical of much that is beautiful and striking in the Devonian landscape. To the north the verdant Exe Valley (beloved of fishermen) stretches in almost a direct line to Dulverton and the uplands of Exmoor, the haunt of the red-deer and the home of those quaint specimens of humanity described in the novels of R. D. Blackmore. Southwards lies Topsham, the trysting-place of the hardy adventurers of Elizabethan times, and the fruitful plain through which both the Exe, and the water-way which follows its course at a

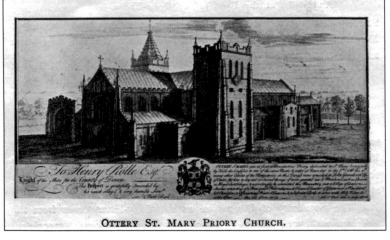

OTTERY ST. MARY PRIORY CHURCH.

Old guide books are a useful insight into what contemporaries thought of a town or locality. The railway companies issued many such guides, as this example from Devon: the Shire of the Sea Kings, *published by the Great Western Railway in 1908.*

WHERE THE RECORDS ARE

Books may not be able to answer the queries you have, or may stimulate other questions. This means having to look at original material, which can prove to be time consuming (but deeply addictive and rewarding). Most original documents can be found in one of three places: a county record office, a local studies library or a national repository. Directory enquiries should have their phone numbers.

Alternatively there are several guides to record offices, the most comprehensive of which is Janet Foster and Julia Sheppard, *British archives: A Guide to Archive Resources in the United Kingdom* (4th edition, Macmillan, 2001). Others which give addresses and phone numbers are: Ian Mortimer (ed), *Record Repositories in Great Britain* (10th edition, PRO Publications, 1998) and Jeremy Gibson and Pamela Peskett, *Record Offices and How to Find Them* (7th edition, Federation of Family History Societies, 1998). It is important to use the most up to date guide possible, as record offices are always on the move and seem to be constantly changing their phone numbers.

If you have access to the internet there is a website that lists almost all the collections of records held by local record offices. It is maintained by the **National Register of Archives** at *www.hmc.gov.uk* and this database is a very useful tool to see who has what.

COUNTY RECORD OFFICES

Every county has a county record office: a few cities, such as Southampton or Coventry, also have a city archive as well. These record offices hold material created by local government, such as rate books, quarter session records or council minutes, and unofficial material donated by individuals, companies or clubs, which may include such things as land and house deeds, account books, and photographs. Each archive's holdings are very different, so a comprehensive collection of material for one locality may be missing for its neighbour.

It is important to ring beforehand to book a seat as most record offices have very cramped reading areas. They should also be able to give you a rough idea whether they have the records you are interested in. These may only be available on microfiche or microfilm, so you will have to book a reader. If you have not used a record office before, find out before you go what rules they have about providing identification, using lockers for your property, last ordering times and so on. They will be happy to send you a beginner's guide.

Each record office has a different system of managing its records, although they all follow the same principles of archive administration. Documents are kept together by collection, rather than rearranged by subject as happens in a library. A box of solicitor's records, for example, may well contain material on a variety of subjects, from land deeds to company records and individuals' diaries. In a library the collection would be broken up and the land deeds added to other land deeds in the library's possession. This does not happen in an archive.

All this could be very confusing, but fortunately help is at hand. A number of record offices produce leaflets on aspects of the records that can be very useful. These are now often available via their websites.

Most record offices have card indexes arranged by subjects which describe individual items, thus all references to charities or a particular village are kept together. A few counties, notably Essex and Surrey, have computerised catalogues to their holdings, and these are available via their websites. In addition the Access to Archives (A2A) project in England and Wales is providing computerised catalogues to aspects of the holdings of local record offices, such as quarter session records. These new indexes are maintained by the Public Record Office, and can be visited at their website (*www.pro.gov.uk/a2a*).

Instead of directly giving you a unique reference to an individual document these catalogues and indexes may refer you to document lists, which describe what each collection holds. As these lists can give you more detail about individual items within the collection they are worth looking out for.

LOCAL STUDIES LIBRARIES

Local studies libraries are the poor relations of the archive world, mainly because they are neither quite an archive nor really a library but contain elements of both. They are likely to have a comprehensive collection of books about the locality, including street directories. From an archival point of view their greatest asset is often a comprehensively indexed collection of press cuttings from local, and sometimes national, newspapers going back to before the First World War. They may well also have some original documents, such as poor law records or personal papers, but they are usually not the first place to see original material.

It can be difficult to locate local studies libraries. They are normally part of the central reference library. Many are listed in Foster and Shepherd's *British archives: a guide to archive resources in the United Kingdom.* Those with access to the internet can find some addresses through the Familia website *(www.earl.org.uk/familia2).*

THINK LOCALLY, RESEARCH NATIONALLY

Most local historians would not think of using the great national repositories during their researches. But there may be surprisingly useful material at the Public Record Office, the Family Records Centre, and the British Library. A quick rule of thumb is that local record offices hold records of local government, people and business. The Public Record Office and other national repositories have records of national significance. If you are still not sure a quick phone call to the archive will normally provide an answer.

The **Public Record Office** (PRO) is the national archive for the United Kingdom and England and Wales. It is by far and away the biggest archive in the British Isles, storing over a hundred miles of

The Public Record Office (PRO) is Britain's national archive. It has much of interest to local historians from the Domesday Book to plans for housing and road schemes in the 1960s.

documents: the average local record office will hold no more than half a mile of records. For the local historian there is a mass of material from medieval land records to files on traffic schemes of the 1960s. And there are sets of tithe, enclosure and valuation maps which might make up gaps at local record offices.

Finding the information you want is not difficult but it can be time consuming, although there are both guides and knowledgeable staff to help. The Office's website *www.pro.gov.uk* is also very useful as it contains an on-line electronic catalogue to the whole of the Office's holdings and downloadable leaflets about many of the records. The PRO will be publishing a guide to its holdings for local historians probably during 2002.

The **Family Records Centre** is a joint venture between the PRO and the Office for National Statistics. On the ground floor it holds the registers of births, marriages and deaths which used to be at St Catherine's House and before that at Somerset House. On the first floor are a complete set of census returns for England and Wales between 1841 and 1891, an invaluable source for anybody studying Victorian towns and villages. Copies of Prerogative Court of Canterbury **wills** – a useful source in building up a picture of local wealth and property ownership – can also be found there.

Unlike the PRO and the FRC, the **British Library** (BL) does not really welcome non-academic readers. They will normally only give you a reader's ticket if you can prove that the material you want to see is to be found nowhere else. That said, the British Library has the largest collection of books and manuscripts in the country, (the catalogue is on-line at *www.bl.uk2)*. Other copyright libraries, which should hold copies of all published books, are the Bodleian in Oxford, Cambridge University Library, and the National Library of Wales, Aberystwyth. The BL's manuscript collection is equally impressive with a vast hotchpotch of material from medieval land deeds to the papers of modern politicians. It also runs the **British Library Newspaper Library** which has copies of most newspapers, magazines and journals ever published in Britain.

Most university libraries, outside London, welcome serious researchers who are not registered students. A simple phone call will tell you how to get access. Their holdings may well include books unavailable elsewhere. It is becoming fairly easy to find what each university library holds as their catalogues are now generally available on-line, so you can get a pretty good idea of what is available before you get there.

There are hundreds of archives that have records which could help you in your research. As well as local record offices, many universities and museums have archives which may be worth exploring.

Another surprisingly useful source for local historians is the **Society of Genealogists**, whose library has a fine collection of material on local history, (the library's catalogue is available on the internet at *www.sog.org.uk2*). A fee, currently £3 per hour or £12 per day, is charged for non-members to use the Library. An article about the value of the Society's holdings to local historians can be found in issue 78 (March-April 2000) of *Local History Magazine*.

UNDERTAKING RESEARCH

Local history is a detective story. And like every good detective you must discover the facts and present them in a convincing way. You must therefore be methodical and accurate in your research. It also helps to be critical of the sources, to understand what was in the mind of the person as they put pen to paper, the arguments they were putting forward and the reasons for any omissions. This is important, for example, in reading old newspapers, which were often partisan supporters of one political party or another and thus skewed what they were reporting (particularly local controversies) along party lines.

USING WRITTEN SOURCES

Written sources are the basis of local history. Using them properly makes the best use of your time and ensures that you get all you can from the records. You should do the following:

- Note down all the references of the documents you consult, together with their descriptions, even for those items which were useless. You may need to use them again; having the references can cut the work in half.
- Read each document thoroughly, especially if you are unfamiliar with the type of record. See whether there is an index at the front or back which could help.
- Many records come in similar form. One will, for example, is much like another. Once you have mastered the style they are easier to go through. The form may well remain the same whether the document is in Latin or English.
- There may be an index or other finding aid. Ask the staff.
- If you are not sure about how to use a document or reading it, ask the staff. They are there to help!

- Note down everything of interest in PENCIL (record offices will not allow use of pens or biros) together with the reference of the document in a notebook. Try to keep your notes legible.
- Put your name and address in notebooks. If you lose them some kind soul may return them to you.

MAKING USE OF YOUR RESEARCH

Although research is a deeply satisfying pastime in itself, you should aim to write up your study and publish it in some way, so that other people can make use of your work (think how you benefited from the research of others) and admire your perspicacity! There are three main ways of doing this:

- Book or pamphlet. You may be able to persuade the local history society to publish your work, alternatively you can either publish the book yourself or approach a publisher to do it for you. Whatever you do, you are unlikely to make a profit. There are several excellent books on the subject, including Bob Trubshaw's *How to Write and Publish Local History* (Heart of Albion Press, 1999) and David Dymond's *Researching and Writing History: A Practical Guide for Local Historians* (British Association for Local History, 1999).
- Submit an article to a local history journal. Editors welcome well-written, interesting contributions. Don't make it too long. Two or three thousand words is the maximum length most editors will consider.
- Putting your research on the internet is an increasingly popular alternative. It is almost free and there is literally a world-wide audience waiting to read what you've written, although it is not as easy to create an attractive site that people will want to come back to as it might seem at first glance. Most internet service providers (ISP) will display your webpages for free. It is surprisingly easy to do (even for technical novices, like myself as you can see by logging on to *www.sfowler.force9.co.uk*). There are a number of books and internet magazines which can help you, as well as sites on the internet itself.

3
POPULATION AND PEOPLE: LIFE AND WORK

●●●●●

The physical evidence of how people have lived over the centuries lies all around us. Population growth may have led to the building of new estates and streets of housing. Indeed, whole new suburbs may have been built to house new arrivals. Occupations may result in specific buildings, not just warehouses and factories, but buildings adapted to new roles. Larger houses usually, but not always, denote middle and upper class areas, although the real difference may be in the quality of the craftsmanship and architecture. Conversely, mean streets of back-to-back factory workers' houses may have survived the slum clearance programmes of the 1950s and 1960s.

It can be more difficult to trace improvements in public health on the ground, but look out for old bath houses and waterworks (often a splendid Victorian building) or you may able to identify a pestilent marshy area which was once drained to rid the area of fever.

A good introduction to many of the topics covered in this chapter is Colin D. Rogers and John M. Smith, *Local Family History in England* (Manchester University Press, 1991).

POPULATION CHANGE

Although it is natural to assume that the population has always been rising, it certainly is not the case. The population fell considerably after the Black Death in the mid-14th century and probably declined during the economic depression in the first half of the 17th.

Large population increases really began with the onset of the **industrial and agricultural revolutions** in the late 18th century, although nobody really knows why. The industrial revolution drew people from rural areas into new mill and factory towns, thus leading to a decline in the population of many agricultural areas, particularly in the south of England. Many people, for example, left rural Somerset to find work across the Bristol Channel in the forges and mines of South Wales. Even today there is migration from the North to the South East, ironically reversing the pattern of 150 years, resulting in increased building in towns across the region and the creation of new towns such as Milton Keynes.

The reason for much of this migration was, and is, economic – work and the chance of better prospects. Occasionally there was a personal reason to move, such as a marriage partner or the desire to escape from personal commitments. Conversely many families remained rooted to a particular village or district and family members rarely moved outside a narrow area.

It can be difficult to trace migratory patterns. The **Census** Enumerators Books, between 1851 and 1901, include information about the place where people were born, so it is possible to work out where incomers came from. Occasionally you may find that in large families each child was born in a different place, which again can give some idea of how people moved around.

Migrants often set up social clubs and other organisations to help new arrivals within their community. In the larger towns there may be a Welsh chapel, a Scottish Burns Society, and Irish and Jewish charities. Where records for these bodies survive they can offer an insight into the problems faced by migrants. Curiously, migrants from English districts rarely formed formal associations of this kind.

One subject we are never likely to know very much about is what went on between the sheets of the 19th and early 20th century bedrooms. It is well known that Victorian families were often very large – six to eight children were by no means uncommon, although high infant mortality might lead to the deaths of two or three in childhood. The size of families however dropped after 1870, although nobody is quite sure why. This decline seems to have been common across all social classes. Perhaps couples practised abstinence, or birth control was more widely available than is assumed.

Illegitimacy rates also fell during the 19th and first half of the 20th century. The rural custom or expectation, in some parts of the country, that the bride should be pregnant on her wedding day was firmly suppressed. Instead there grew up a belief in purity and chastity, which made it a sin for a woman to go to the altar other than as a virgin. Yet it

The provision of social welfare can also be a fruitful subject for the local historian. Workhouse records are often plentiful and can illuminate the conditions endured by the residents. Here elderly inmates at St Pancras Workhouse in London enjoy a frugal meal.

is by no means certain that it was as widely practised as we might believe. Certainly prostitution was a particular problem in many Victorian cities, and evidence from social workers during the First World War suggests that many working class couples cohabited. It is however rare to pick up evidence in the **census**, as few prostitutes are identified as such and it is hard to identify unmarried mothers or cohabiting couples.

Many illegitimate children were born in the workhouse and cared for by **poor law** authorities, and records and registers often survive. However, the survival of records for charity nursing homes and orphanages is much less certain, although Barnados and one or two other children's charities maintain good records. Between 1844 and 1858 magistrates had to submit returns of bastards born in their districts and these returns can sometimes be found in Petty Session records at local record offices. Before 1834 there are also bastardy and settlement papers in **quarter session** records which can be illuminating.

34

THEMES YOU MIGHT CONSIDER PURSUING

- The growth of a particular suburb or village. What factors were there in its growth or decline during the period you are interested in?
- Migration into a district. Did the town act as a magnet drawing people from the local district in or did new residents come from farther afield?
- More difficult is the study of emigration, largely because there are few official records. Where did people from your district move to in Britain and overseas, and what reasons were there for their choice?
- What was the class structure of the district, and how did this change over time? It can be particularly difficult working out who was middle-class and who was working-class, although a number of local history textbooks offer some advice on how to proceed.
- Where did people from particular social classes live in your district and did this change? It is generally assumed that over time the middle and upper classes moved to newer and healthier districts on the outskirts of towns – did this happen in your district?
- The changing size of families. What was the decline in your area, and was it differentiated by class? Did working class families continue to have larger families longer than their middle class and upper class contemporaries?

OCCUPATIONS

Many towns and rural areas have a long connection with a particular trade or industry. Buckinghamshire was, for example, long known for its lace making which was largely undertaken by women and children at home. Birmingham and Sheffield had specialist districts dedicated to jewellery and cutlery making, while women made chains in the Black Country.

Of course, it was rare for a district to be totally dominated by one industry; even in mining villages there were likely to have been shop-owners and farmers. And mining itself would have been divided into dozens of different specialisms, from the men at the coal face and their assistants to the people who looked after the pit ponies and the pithead baths as well as various grades of foremen and supervisors.

The great changes in British society since the end of the Second World War have seen many traditional trades swept away, as mines and factories closed, to be replaced by new forms of light industry. Over

Any general history of a district should take into account local industries. Coventry, for example, developed rapidly in the first half of the twentieth century as a centre of the motor industry. This view is of the erecting shop at the Daimler Motor Works at about the time of the First World War.

the past two centuries agriculture has been increasingly mechanised which resulted in the decline of many traditional skills and crafts.

The growth and decline of these occupations is a fruitful subject for the local historian. Why did the trade grow here? How was the work undertaken? Who worked in the industry? What caused its decline? These are all questions that can be tackled.

Fortunately there are many sources at hand to help the researcher. The first thing to do is to see whether there are already books on the subject. Staff in the local history or reference libraries should be able to point you in the right direction. Another useful source of published material is contemporary accounts of the industry. If you are very lucky there may be diaries and reminiscences of some of the people who actually undertook the work. One of the best known is Alfred Williams, *Life in a Railway Factory* (Sutton, 1984) which describes the railway works at Swindon in the years before the First World War. There may also be accounts of the industry or trade written by outsiders. George Orwell's famous account of mining, for example, brilliantly describes the experience of going underground in the 1930s, and there are many accounts of life on the railways.

There may be more analytical accounts, particularly for London. During the 1850s, for example, the journalist Henry Mayhew interviewed people in many trades and selections of his work have often been republished, including as *London Labour and the London Poor* by Penguin in 1985. Forty years later Charles Booth studied the poor in London and descriptions of the work they undertook and the conditions they worked in appear in his *Life and Labour of the People in London* (Macmillan, 1903). These books are much more hard to come by, but there is a website (*http://booth.lse.ac.uk*) which contains information which may help. A similar study was undertaken in York by Seebohm Rowntree. Even if your interest lies outside the metropolis these books may give a flavour of what conditions were like in the trade or industry you are studying. Librarians should be able to tell you about similar accounts for your area.

Occupations, particularly those regarded as injurious to health or

Social reformers need not always be national figures. Sarah Martin, a poor dressmaker in Great Yarmouth, did much to improve conditions in the local prisons in the 1820s and 1830s.

Women workers could become the main stay of local industries, as varied as chain making in the Black Country and strawplaiting in rural Buckinghamshire. The inter-war period saw the expansion of light industry, which employed many women. Here girls pack light bulbs at the Osram Factory.

employing women and children, have often been the subject of official enquiries. They may well have been published as a **Parliamentary Paper** and include evidence from the workers themselves as well as figures in the industry, together with written submissions which can build up an overall picture. Another useful source is the monthly *Board of Trade Labour Gazette* (from 1920 the *Ministry of Labour Gazette*), which reported regularly on labour conditions. Sets of these gazettes are at the **Public Record Office** and the Modern Records Centre, University of Warwick, Coventry CV4 7AL (*http://modernrecords.warwick.ac.uk*). Other university libraries may have sets.

If you are interested in which industries or trades were important in your area the first place to start is the **census** records. You should look at the original enumerators books (on microfilm or fiche) which give a house-by-house breakdown of what people did. The published census reports found in **Parliamentary Papers** are also worth checking as they break down occupations in counties and larger towns. Street **directories** may well list local employers and shops. Many also give the occupations of local householders as well.

There may be **business records** either at local record offices or elsewhere. The PRO for example has the majority of the records of the pre-nationalisation railway companies. Trade union records may also be important. The largest collection is at the Modern Records Centre. The Working Class Movement Library, 51 The Crescent, Salford M5 4WX (*www.wcml.org.uk*) also has sizable holdings.

Other useful sources are trade journals and magazines. By the end of the 19th century most industries and occupations had such publications, which can tell you a lot about conditions faced by trades and the people working in them. The **British Library Newspaper Library** holds the largest collection of journals although local studies libraries or record offices may hold journals relating to major industries locally. Local **newspapers** will include stories about local businesses and the people who worked in them.

It can be more difficult to find physical evidence of occupations. Occasionally buildings may have been specially built or converted to enable work at home to take place. The houses of silk weavers for example had extra large windows on the first floor to allow natural light to reach the weaving machines. Sometimes you may find a maze of narrow streets full of small workshops – such as the Jewellery Quarter in Birmingham. More often found are mills and factories, many now derelict or converted to other purposes.

THEMES YOU MIGHT CONSIDER PURSUING

- The history of a local trade or occupation.
- The importance a trade, occupation or industry had for the local economy and society.
- A particular incident, such as a mining accident or strike.
- An **oral history** project with former workers, particularly if the industry or trade is no longer in operation.
- An **industrial archaeological** survey of former buildings and sites connected with a local industry or trade. Seek professional guidance however before you start on a project of this kind.
- In rural areas you might want to look at the changing nature of farming, perhaps by tracing the history of a particular farm or crop.

SOCIAL CONDITIONS

Life for many people in both the new industrial towns and the more established urban communities could be appalling. Housing was often grim, with cellars and single rooms given over to housing whole families. Although more picturesque, rural housing was often no better. Food was rarely adequate and often adulterated. Health care, for the poor at least, was rudimentary. And in many working class households there was continual worry about getting and retaining work – unemployment could lead to destitution. But perhaps the worse aspect of all was sanitation – providing fresh water and getting rid of waste. Without these basic services, disease killed thousands of people each year.

From the late 18th century, and especially after the passing of the Public Health Act in 1848, much effort was made by local authorities, beginning with ad hoc bodies of **Improvement Commissioners**, eventually followed by **borough** and city councils with new powers to clear slums and lay drainage. Birmingham, under Joseph Chamberlain, was the most famous proponent of what came to be known as 'gas and water socialism', although smaller authorities could also pioneer new developments. Richmond, in Surrey had one of the first public libraries in the country as well as building an early council housing estate.

The 20th century saw extensive slum clearance and the consequent construction of council estates and even new towns to house the overspill from cities.

Fortunately these appalling living conditions were well documented and can make a fascinating, if occasionally stomach turning, study. Again the best way to start is to see what has already been published, either by historians or at the time.

Many contemporary journalists, writers and social scientists wrote about conditions in working class areas. Many districts of most large towns and cities probably had books, articles or newspaper accounts written about them, although they can now be difficult to track down. The East End of London was a favourite place to visit. The most famous of these accounts are probably Friedrich Engels, *The Condition of the Working Class in England* (1845) about Manchester and William Booth's *In Darkest England and the Way Out* (1890) on London. Amongst accounts still in print is Henry Mayhew, *London Labour and London Life* first published in 1865 (Penguin, 1985), Maud Pember Reeves, *Round About a Pound a Week* (Virago, 1979) first published in 1913 about life in Lambeth, and Robert Roberts, *The Classic Slum: Salford Life in the First Quarter of the Century* (Pelican, 1978).

Even small towns had slum areas, as this illustration from a newspaper article of 1897 about Richmond shows. Much of the area was demolished before the First World War and the remainder are now desirable middle class homes!

Another useful source are the **Parliamentary Papers**, for there were a number of royal commissions and other enquiries into social conditions. One of the most famous was the *Report on the Sanitary Conditions of the Labouring Population of Great Britain* (1842) which found that the effect of deaths caused by 'epidemic, endemic and contagious diseases' each year was as if the 'whole county of Huntingdonshire, or any equivalent district, were entirely depopulated annually.'

There may well also be local enquiries and surveys. Some of the first were local reports to the General Board of Health, which were undertaken in a number of towns (but not London) between 1848 and 1857, which often make deeply depressing reading. The largest collection of these reports is in the Chadwick Papers at the **British Library**, otherwise their survival is patchy. For more information see the essay in L.M. Munby, *Short Guides to Records: First Series* (Historical Association, 1994).

The records of Medical Officers of Health are often an important source, as they had the power to investigate public health matters and make recommendations on how to improve matters. Annual reports on their work and the state of public health, can make fascinating reading. Their survival is patchy, but they may sometimes be found at local studies libraries or record offices.

As the responsibility for improving social conditions fell largely with local authorities it is these records you will need to consult. Most established permanent committees, or ad hoc sub-committees perhaps dealing with slum clearance. Surviving records should include minutes and reports made to meetings, and if you are lucky some of the accompanying paperwork and files may also have been kept. These records should be at the county record office, although there may be restrictions on looking at more recent material.

Other records which are likely to be of use are:

- **Census** records, the published reports may contain general statistics about overcrowding. Going through the census enumerators' books will give an insight into what overcrowding and poor conditions meant for actual families.

The signs of Victorian town improvements are to be found all around us – but they are not always obvious. Richmond's Public Library, which opened in 1881, was the first to be paid for by local government.

- **Newspapers** are an important source, because they may well expose poor conditions locally and contain reports and stories about slum clearance and the improvement of public health. Letters columns are also worth reading for the views, sometimes staggeringly stupid, of the paper's readers.
- **Photographs** can show you what the area looked like before public health schemes were implemented, how the improvements were made, and what the final result looked like.
- **Maps and plans** may accompany reports on sanitary conditions or exist for slum clearance schemes and new housing. Again they are useful evidence on the problems which faced councils and the steps they took to improve matters.

Evidence on the ground can be hard to find, but very rewarding when you come across something. You may discover, for example, a row of model working class dwellings or an early council housing scheme. The worst 19th century slums seem to have been in courts and passageways leading off main roads, so it is worth looking out for surviving buildings of this kind – although it may be difficult now to visualise conditions in them 150 years ago. Street furniture is another useful guide: perhaps the lamp posts are the originals, or there are 'stink pipes' which vented noxious gases from the sewers beneath. Most of the general introductions to local history (see Appendix II) include something on this subject. Of particular interest is Kate Tiller, *English Local History: an Introduction* (Sutton, 2001).

THEMES YOU MIGHT CONSIDER PURSUING

- The history of a particular scheme, say a housing estate or a new sewer.
- A survey of social provision at a certain time. What was it like to live in your town or village in, say, 1801, 1851 or 1901?
- Housing or poverty in a particular district and the attempts made to improve matters.
- Biographies of the men (and a few women) who were instrumental in clearing the slums and laying the sewers.

4
SOCIAL LIFE: PUBS, CLUBS AND CHARITIES

•••••

The gathering of people together, usually but certainly not always men, has long been a feature of English life, whether in the pub or the club, or more formally in self-improvement societies or charitable good works. It is only in the past few years that local historians have begun to explore this rich historical strand, so it is a subject that cries out for research.

Although inns and taverns have been around since medieval times, the first shoots of organised recreational life appeared in the period after the Restoration in 1660. Group social activities flourished in the 18th and 19th centuries, perhaps coming to their peak in the years before the First World War. Provincial theatres and assembly rooms were a feature of the 18th century, while the period after 1800 saw social clubs, sports clubs, the music hall and charities flourish, partly because the working classes began to have increased leisure time. Towns, such as Bath and Blackpool, grew up to cater for people's leisure needs. Since the Second World War many such activities have been under threat from television and a variety of new leisure pursuits. Even so, charities and many societies, such as those devoted to local and family history, thrive.

One difficulty that researchers in this field have is the paucity of archival material, as relatively few internal records of theatres, clubs and charities, let alone public houses have survived. Often evidence has to be pieced together from other sources. **Directories**, for example, may include lists of local societies, theatres, charities and public houses. Their activities are likely to be covered in some detail in local **newspapers**. Neither of the above sources are likely to describe more informal or working class clubs, such as allotment or pig clubs, and so it might be almost impossible to find out much about such societies. Using **oral history** techniques it may still be possible, just, to record the memories of pre-war members of societies.

Surviving physical evidence is also patchy. Many theatres, pubs and chapels (which themselves were the centre of many social activities) survive either engaged in the activities for which they were built, or still recognisable as such even if change of use has occurred. You may also come across Masonic halls and social clubs. It is always worth checking to see whether there is a foundation stone, which may tell you when the building was begun and who laid the stone or performed the opening ceremony.

It is impossible to describe here the rich variety of associational life, which almost every town had, from choral societies to Turkish baths. Instead I have concentrated on three important spheres: the public house, the charity, and the friendly society. At the end I have given information about one or two other areas worthy of possible study. There are however many other organised social activities – such as sports or the theatre – which for want of space have not been included

So many old theatres, music halls and cinemas have been lost, which is a great pity because they are of great architectural interest and importance for local history. This is Richmond Theatre, built in the 1890s and recently lovingly restored.

45

Football, in particular, became very popular with working class men and boys in industrial areas. Reports of matches, and often the accompanying trouble, fill local newspapers. This is an unidentified team – winners of the Lancashire FA Challenge Cup, sometime in the 1890s. (Courtesy: Miss J. Sharples)

here. If you are interested in pursuing such subjects there is often a rich literature produced by enthusiasts, which can be tracked down via a library or increasingly over the internet.

THEMES YOU MIGHT CONSIDER PURSUING

- The history of a particular institution, such as a club, pub, theatre or charity. Don't forget to set any history in context, comparing your subject with like bodies in the neighbourhood as well as with national developments.
- The growth, change and (where appropriate) decline of, for example, amateur dramatics or a particular sport, in a district.
- The people who were involved running a club, charity or staffing a pub.
- Aspects of organised social life unique to the district, such as a fair, festival or annual parade.

FURTHER READING

Peter Clark, *British Clubs and Societies 1580-1800: The Origins of an Associational World* (Clarendon Press, 2000) is a comprehensive account of the development of clubs and societies. Sadly nothing as good exists for the period after 1800, although Stephen Yeo, *Religion and Voluntary Organisations in Crisis* (Croom Helm, 1976) is a thorough examination of Reading in the years before 1914. There are also chapters on charities and clubs, societies and associations in F.M.L. Thompson (ed), *The Cambridge Social History of Britain, 1750-1950* (Cambridge UP, 1990). A number of local societies and clubs have produced histories, usually to accompany significant anniversaries – copies of which may be held by local studies libraries.

PUBLIC HOUSES

Until recently the public house was the centre of social life outside the home. Over the centuries it has survived threats from the coffee houses of the 17th century, the assembly rooms and gin shops of the 18th, and the music halls and nonconformist chapels of the 19th. So it is not surprising that many friendly societies, athletic and social clubs had pubs as their headquarters in the late 19th century.

Careful examination of the outside of pubs can often reveal signs of their history: two cottages or houses knocked into one, or a pub which has expanded into neighbouring houses or shops, or windows etched with the name of a long defunct brewery. It is usually fairly easy to spot when a building was formerly a pub. Perhaps some tiling remains, or a door is in an odd place, or it was the slightly grander building at the end of a terraced street.

The inside of most pubs has been greatly altered over the years. Since the Second World War the trend has been to knock smaller bars into one, but it is often possible to trace where these once were. There are regional variations in pub architecture. A Northern pub with a narrow corridor leading to a variety of small rooms is uncommon down south. In southern England many pubs traditionally consisted of an entrance to two bars, a saloon and a public bar, with an off-sales point in the middle.

Brewery records are often a good source, although their survival is a bit patchy. Some breweries keep their own records, but many have been deposited at local record offices. The **National Register of**

In most areas public houses were the centre of social activity until well after the Second World War. Here a group pose outside an unidentified Midlands pub, probably in the early 1920s.

Archives should be able to tell where these records are. Young's and Bass are among breweries which maintain their own archives. Brewery records may tell you from whom the pub was bought or when the land it was built on was acquired. There may be material about rebuilding or redecoration, with plans and architects' drawings.

County record offices should hold licensed victuallers' records. From 1552 alehouse keepers had to have the permission of the local justices of the peace to sell beer. Records are often arranged by licensee rather than by the name of the public house. For more information about these records see Jeremy Gibson and Judith Hunter, *Victuallers' Licences* (Federation of Family History Societies, 2000). Record offices may also have auctioneers' records that could give you information about the sale of buildings and adjacent land, who bought the property and how much it was worth.

Other more general sources that may help in your researches are:

Census records
Directories
Maps
Newspapers
Photographs

There are a number of histories of pubs and beer in Britain. The best modern introduction is Peter Haydon, *The English Pub: a History* (Robert Hale, 1994). Occasionally breweries have produced histories of their pubs, such as Helen Osborn, *Inn and Around London: A History of Young's Pubs* (Young's, 1991). There are a number of websites devoted to pub history, including the excellent National Pubs and Breweries website (*www.btinternet.com/~steven.williams1/ pubpgintro.htm*) which has a bulletin board and links to many other sites around the country. Another useful site is the Pubs, Inns and Taverns Index, 1801-1901 (*www.pubsindex.freeserve.co.uk*) which provides an index to the public houses of the 19th century and the people who worked in them.

There is a new Pub History Group which aims to bring historians interested in the public house together for mutual enlightenment and pleasure. To join contact the Secretary c/o 13 Grovewood, Sandycombe Road, Richmond TW9 3NF or visit the web site at (*www.uk-history.co.uk/phs.htm*).

CHARITIES

The earliest charities go back nearly 900 years. One of the earliest is the Hospital of St Cross in Winchester which was founded by Bishop Henry de Blois, a grandson of William the Conqueror, in 1136. The Hospital still looks after old people and provides bread and ale to passing travellers who demand it.

Until the 19th century charities were largely established as the result of bequests made in the wills of the rich. As a result most towns have an almshouse or two housing the elderly. Many grammar and public schools were also established in a similar way.

Charities grew up indiscriminately. The City of London and cathedral and market towns were often well provided for, while the new industrial towns of Lancashire and Yorkshire had very few such

The earliest almshouses are medieval. They form a little known link with the past, both in the surviving buildings and the records, which may go back centuries. This photograph is of Hickey's Almshouses in Richmond – the buildings were constructed in the 1850s but consciously look back to the medieval period.

charities. By the mid-19th century these endowed charities were largely an anachronism, even if they remained important locally.

Towards the end of the 18th century there was a great revival of interest in charities. But their organisation took a new form, for they now largely depended on subscriptions and donations, and were run by a committee elected (although usually self-appointing) from amongst the subscribers. They varied greatly in size and function. The largest were national institutions, such as the RSPCA, which by the end of the 19th century had nearly 150 branches and over a thousand local auxiliaries. Local charities might only have a couple of dozen subscribers and donors.

These charities were a way for middle-class women to find a respectable occupation outside the home, giving many self-confidence and the feeling of achievement at a time when such opportunities were limited. By the end of the 19th century, perhaps 500,000 women regularly took part in some form of voluntary activity each week, and another 20,000 were engaged in paid work with one charity or another.

By the First World War the state was beginning to play a greater role in helping the poor. Even so voluntary work remains as important today as it ever was in the past.

It can be very difficult to find records created by charities, partly because there were so many of these bodies and also because so many records have been destroyed. Where they survive, records may be at local record offices, although some of the large national charities, such as the RSPCA or Barnados, have their own archives.

Almost all charities produced an annual report and it is these records which most often survive. They usually included a summary of the year's work, with accounts and lists of committee members and officers, subscribers and donors. Very few records of those who actually helped survive. Occasionally reference to individuals can be found in minute books recording the decisions made by the executive committee and any sub-committees.

The **National Register of Archives** should be able to tell you which charity records survive and where they are to be found. Local study libraries may also have material, as indeed may the charities themselves if they are still in existence.

Other more general sources which could help in your researches are:

Directories
Newspapers

The best historical survey of charities is David Owen, *English Philanthropy, 1660-1960* (Harvard, 1964). Rather shorter is Frank Prochaska, *The Voluntary Impulse: Philanthropy in Modern Britain* (Faber and Faber, 1988) and Norman Alvey, *From Chantry to Oxfam: A Short History of Charities and Charity Legislation* (British Association for Local History, 1996).

The small Voluntary Action History Society, National Centre for Volunteering, Regents Wharf, 8 All Saints St, London N1 9RL (website *www.ivr.org.uk/vahs.htm*) has regular meetings.

FRIENDLY SOCIETIES

Friendly societies were essentially mutual insurance clubs providing cash benefits in cases of injury and sickness, or to dependents on the death of a member. By the end of the 19th century almost every town and village had at least one society.

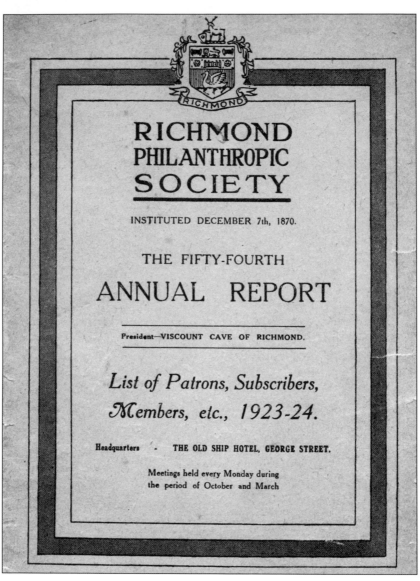

RICHMOND PHILANTHROPIC SOCIETY

INSTITUTED DECEMBER 7th, 1870.

THE FIFTY-FOURTH

ANNUAL REPORT

President—VISCOUNT CAVE OF RICHMOND.

List of Patrons, Subscribers, Members, etc., 1923-24.

Headquarters - THE OLD SHIP HOTEL, GEORGE STREET.

Meetings held every Monday during
the period of October and March

Most local charities produced an annual report, which listed the main subscribers and summarised the work undertaken. Although their survival is somewhat patchy, they can be extremely useful for people interested in social provision. The Richmond Philanthropic Society gave small amounts of money to people in temporary financial distress.

Societies were either independent, or affiliated to larger organisations. Many independent societies date from the 18th century, and perhaps catered for a particular group of workers or were controlled or were run to a degree by local clergymen and other bigwigs. Affiliated societies took off in the 1820s, and were popular because they had financial security as the result of being part of a large organisation. The Ancient Order of Foresters was the largest of these affiliated bodies.

Social activity was another reason for joining. Many societies engaged in some form of harmless ritual based on Masonic rites, which gave members a feeling of belonging. The big event of the year was often a parade to the parish church for a service before sitting down to a large dinner.

National Insurance from 1911 and the Welfare State and the National Health Service in the late 1940s saw the end of most societies, as the services offered were now provided by the state and the social events no longer had the attraction they once did. A small number of friendly societies still survive offering good value financial services.

It is difficult to detect any physical evidence of the existence of these societies, as most met in pubs. A few built their own halls, either singly or acting jointly, but most have long been demolished.

Archival evidence is also patchy. Only about five per cent of records of friendly societies have been deposited in local archives, generally for branches of national friendly societies, rather than for independent local societies. This material often comprises of odd items, which may mean that it will be difficult to research the story of a local friendly society or build up the picture of activity in a particular district.

The most common records are friendly society rulebooks, which give an idea of how societies were run. They are less use for anybody wishing to discover how individual societies changed over time. An almost complete set is at the **Public Record Office**.

Another important series of records are the annual reports produced by the official Registrar of Friendly Societies from 1852 onwards. These reports contain detailed accounts of his work, including details of cases dealt with, and a bewildering array of statistics. Copies are in **Parliamentary Papers**. These Papers also contain other material relating to friendly societies: the most interesting of which are reports and evidence presented to the various investigative commissions and select committees, and surveys. There is, for example, a survey of

1910 listing every society or branch, county by county, with details of membership, assets, income and other information, which is impossible to find elsewhere.

Surviving societies themselves may have records. The Foresters based in Southampton, and the Rechabites in Manchester hold particularly good collections. The **National Register of Archives** has details of records for some 1,700 different friendly societies or branches kept by record offices. Holdings at **local record offices** usually include a scattering of minute and rule books, with the occasional accounts.

Other more general sources which could help in your researches are:

Newspapers
Photographs
Quarter sessions

There is very little written about friendly societies and their records. The first place to start is the article by Audrey Fisk, 'Friendly Societies and Local History' which appeared in the *Local Historian* (Vol 29 no 9 May 1999). It is also available as a separate booklet from the British Association of Local History. Another useful guide is Roger Logan, *Friendly Society Records* (Federation of Family History Societies, 2000). The Ancient Order of Foresters have published a series of leaflets about their records, which are available from the Foresters Heritage Trust, College Place, Southampton SO15 2FE.

A national society encouraging research into all aspects of friendly societies is the Friendly Society Research Group, c/o Faculty of Social Science, Open University, Milton Keynes MK7 6AA (website *www.open.ac.uk/socialsciences/staff/dweinbren*).

5

ECONOMIC DEVELOPMENT: INDUSTRY AGRICULTURE AND TRADE

•••••

For many areas, industrialisation came during the **Industrial Revolution** from 1750 onwards, but industrial activities had long been taking place in a number of towns and villages. For example, paper making prospered in areas of Hertfordshire with fast-running streams or, much more widely, weaving of cloth in East Anglia, or iron smelting in the West Midlands. Existing economic activities such as agriculture, brewing and jewellery making, were often transformed by the introduction of elements of mechanisation, in order to meet increasing demand from a growing population.

It is important to realise that this Revolution took place over at least a century and affected different parts of the country at different times. There seems however to have been a change in about 1850, industrialisation before then often involved small enterprises and resulted in appalling conditions for the workforce. After 1850 factories and companies grew, wages rose and conditions generally improved. The exception was agriculture, which remained depressed and agricultural labourers poorly paid until the First World War.

The twentieth century, of course, saw huge changes, particularly after the 1960s when much heavy industry (steel foundries, coal mines and shipbuilding) closed down in the face of stiff economic competition, to be replaced by new light industries (such as electronics and car parts). Industrialisation continued in areas where new industries, particularly car and aircraft manufacture, grew up, such as Coventry and Hatfield.

It goes without saying that the industrial revolution had a profound affect on local communities. This can make a fruitful study for the local historian, whether looking at a particular industry or how the community as a whole dealt with the changes brought about by industrialisation. Post-war developments can be as interesting as anything that happened centuries ago, with the added advantage that many of the participants are still alive.

The evidence of the industrial revolution lies all around us, whether it be derelict factories and barns or the markets where people have being buying and selling goods for centuries. Indeed a field of study – **industrial archaeology** – has grown up to investigate and catalogue this evidence.

This chapter offers a brief introduction to industrial and agricultural history, as well as mentioning trade and traders.

INDUSTRY

In a work of this size it is impossible to cover all the varieties of industrial activity, from silverware to steel forges. Instead I am going to concentrate on just one – brewing – as a representative to show what records exist and how they can be used in a local history study.

Until the Second World War most towns had one or more breweries. Yet there were also major centres of brewing – Burton-on-Trent and London's East End were perhaps the most important. Brewing originally had been a small scale trade, most households either brewed their own or bought it from the local public house where the publican brewed for customers. Beer was an important drink, for until the introduction of tea and coffee in the 18th century, it was the only beverage which could safely be drunk.

The first large scale commercial breweries were built in the 18th century. Thrale's and Whitbread's breweries in London were among the largest businesses of the day. Because of the special nature of its water, the Staffordshire town of Burton was especially suited for brewing. It also helped that the town had good water connections, which allowed beer to be carried down the Trent for destinations in northern England and export to Europe.

The 19th century saw the spread of commercial breweries and the decline of home-brew pubs, except curiously in parts of the West Midlands. Many of the smaller companies were gradually bought out by larger firms eager to get their hands on their public houses. England was in the almost unique position where the brewers not only made

The image used by the Brewery History Society on its logo shows a typical Victorian tower brewery. As well being very attractive, they were cleverly designed using gravity to speed the brewing process. Working tower breweries can still be seen in Hertford and Lewes, and in the Oxfordshire village of Hook Norton.

beer, but also sold it in premises they owned. The more pubs a brewery owned the more of its beer was likely to be sold. The breweries themselves became more mechanised and many distinctive looking 'tower breweries' were built, a number of which still survive. One of the most attractive is the Harvey's Brewery in Lewes.

Since the end of the Second World War the industry has been in turmoil. Almost all the local breweries have been bought up and their premises closed. Brewing is now largely in the hands of a few multi-national companies. There has however been a resurgence of small breweries ('microbreweries') brewing quality ales for a few pubs or for the free trade.

Because of the scale and nature of brewing there are considerable numbers of sources which can be used in research. Similar material is likely to exist for the history of other industries, and where this is the case this has been indicated.

SECONDARY LITERATURE

Most industries have one or more general histories, which are good places to start for they give an overview of developments and issues which face the historian. Large reference or university libraries should have copies.

For brewing there are two good general histories: Peter Mathias, *The Brewing Industry, 1700-1830* (Cambridge University Press, 1959) and Terry Gourvish and Richard Wilson, *The British Brewing Industry, 1830-1980* (Cambridge University Press, 1984). Welsh breweries are also covered in Brian Glover, *The Prince of Ales* (Sutton Publishing, 1998). There are also a number of histories of individual breweries, usually marking a notable anniversary. Again, long-established companies in other industries may also commission histories. They can be hard to track down, but a good place to start is the local studies library. The Business Archives Council (for details see below) also has a large collection of these histories which can be consulted by appointment.

MUSEUMS

Local museums may have displays about local industries as well as collections of artefacts and ephemera which are not on show. There are also a number of museums which specialise in aspects of industrial history or particular industries. The most important brewery museum, for example, is the Bass Museum in Burton, which collects equipment, records and advertising about the Bass brewery and the companies which it has taken over in the past 200 years. Museums have curators who may be able to help answer specific questions about the industry or the equipment used.

SOCIETIES

If you become interested in researching aspects of a particular trade or industry it is worth joining a society dedicated to its study. Most such societies publish a regular journal or newsletter and organise other events. They may also have produced books and guides to help members. The Brewery History Society publishes a list of 20th century breweries, plus an increasing number of more detailed county guides to all known brewers. Societies are a very good way to learn more about the subject and meet fellow enthusiasts. They can however be difficult to track down, although most now have a presence on the internet. Many addresses are also given in the annual *Genealogical Services Directory: Family and Local History Handbook.*

ARCHIVES

Most large companies appoint archivists or records managers to look after their historic material. They are normally willing to answer simple questions and make archives available to researchers. Breweries which have archivists include Guinness, Bass and Young's. Similarly, the former nationalised industries often have an archives centre or museum, such as the National Gas Archive, Common Lane Partington, Manchester M31 4BR (*www.bg-group.com/archive*). In general however, archive or record management sections can be difficult to track down, so it is normally best to begin by contacting the public relations department.

The sort of material available may include company minutes, accounts, correspondence, staff registers and share-records together with ephemera (particularly in breweries). There may however be restrictions on what you can see.

The records of many companies have been deposited at public repositories. The Modern Records Centre, University of Warwick, Coventry CV4 7Al (*www.modernrecords.warwick.co.uk*) has material for many large companies. Some professional bodies also collect papers of members and the companies they worked for. Most **county record offices** have the records of a number of local companies – their completeness varies. The **National Register of Archives** should be able to tell which records are held by which local record office.

The Business Archives Council, 10 Whitechapel High St, London E1 7RE, telephone: 020 7247 0024 (*www.archives.gla.ac.uk/bac/*) has undertaken surveys of records of particular industries. Those for banking, brewing, chartered accountancy, shipbuilding and the archives of the 1,000 oldest registered companies in Britain have been published. Copies can be often found in large libraries or at local record offices.

OTHER RECORDS WHICH MIGHT BE OF USE

Census – lists employees and their families. Employers are often identified by the number of men they employ.

Directories – will give you an idea of the industrial enterprises in the area, where they operated and a rough impression of when firms started (that is, first appear) and closed down (when they no longer appear). There are also many industry-wide directories listing firms and suppliers in the industry, such as *Kelly's Directory of the Brewing, Wine and Spirit Trades*.

Maps and plans – large-scale maps will show where companies were based and may indicate the location of individual buildings.

Newspapers – local newspapers should include stories about firms, such as features about company outings or annual dinners, strikes, the building of new premises or indeed closure. Another useful source is trade journals – most industries had one or more which may well include articles about the people and developments in your local area.

Oral history – the memories of employees (and their managers) can often bring alive the feeling of what it was like to work in trades and industries which have perhaps long closed, in a way that archival research cannot.

Photographs – again are another way of showing what life was like, as well as developments over the years such as new buildings or machinery.

THEMES YOU MIGHT CONSIDER PURSUING

- The growth and development of a particular industry in your area. Why was the industry attracted to the district – perhaps there were suitable natural resources, good communications, or a ready market for the products?
- The structure of the industry. Was it dominated by large companies or were there a number of small workshops? Did consolidation take place over time and what brought this about?
- Technical developments over time within the industry.
- Where did the people who worked in the industry come from, how did they develop the skills needed to carry out their work? How about labour relations – was the workforce unionised, were there strikes or other industrial action?
- What about the eventual decline of the industry? What caused it, and what was the impact on the local community?

THE STRIKE OF COLLIERS IN DURHAM.

OAKENSHAW, ONE OF THE VILLAGES WHERE THE PITMEN WERE EJECTED FROM THEIR COTTAGES.

GREAT MEETING OF PITMEN ON THE BATTS, BISHOP AUCKLAND.—SEE PRECEDING PAGE.

Industrial relations can make an interesting study for local historians. The minefields have a long heritage of bitter industrial disputes. These pictures from the Illustrated London News *of November 1863, show a strike of pitmen at Oakenshaw near Durham.*

AGRICULTURE

Until the 1850s the majority of people lived on the land and, for centuries, agriculture was the most important source of wealth within the British economy. Despite set-backs during the century or so after the Black Death and for much of the seventeenth century, British prosperity depended to a great extent on the land.

The period after 1750 saw an **agricultural revolution** to match that of industry. The introduction of new machinery and techniques coupled with the rationalisation of land ownership (**enclosure**) led to an increase in productivity which could feed the growing population as a whole. This revolution was achieved at considerable human cost as the new machines needed far fewer hands to operate them. Those who remained on the land lived in picturesque poverty as their wages were low, particularly after the 1870s when cheap imports of food depressed agriculture in general. It took the two world wars (particularly the

Second) to restore prosperity to the industry with a deliberate government policy to encourage home grown food production.

SECONDARY LITERATURE

There are a large number of books on British agricultural history. The most comprehensive guide, if perhaps a little daunting, is the eight volumes of the Agrarian History of England and Wales published by the Cambridge University Press. For the period after 1750 see J.D. Chambers and G.E. Mingay, *The Agricultural Revolution, 1750-1880* (Batsford, 1966). G.E. Mingay is also the author of *Rural Life in Victorian England* (Heinneman, 1977, 2nd edition 1990). Pamela Horn has written many books about rural life in Victorian and Edwardian England, which are both very readable and informative, including *The Changing Countryside in Victorian and Edwardian England* (Athlone, 1984) and *Life and Labour in Rural England, 1700-1850* (Macmillan, 1987). There are a number of eye-witness accounts of rural life including, of course, Flora Thompson's famous book *Lark Rise to Candleford* and various books by George Ewart Evans including *Ask the Fellows who Cut the Hay* (Faber, 1962).

A number of books look at the rural landscape, notably W.G. Hoskins' *Making of the English Landscape* (Penguin Books, 1970) and Richard Muir's *The New Guide to Reading the Landscape: Fieldwork in Local History* (Exeter University Press, 2000).

MUSEUMS

There are several museums of rural life. The largest and oldest is the Museum of English Rural Life which is part of the University of Reading's Rural History Centre. The Centre has a comprehensive collection of artefacts and archival material on rural history. The address of both the Museum and Centre is PO Box 229, Whiteknights, Reading RG6 6AG (*www.rdg.ac.uk/insts/im/*). In Wales, the Museum of Welsh Life, St. Fagans, Cardiff, CF5 6XB (*www.nmgw.ac.uk/mwl*) also has large collections of material relating to rural life in the principality.

ARCHIVES

Archives of farms and the great estates can sometimes be found at

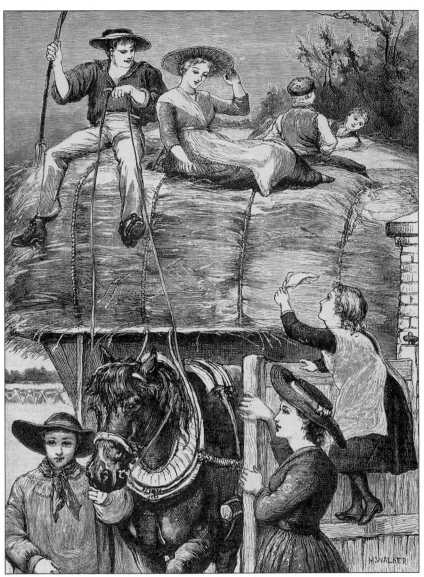

A sentimentalised Victorian view of bringing the harvest home. Unfortunately the reality was very different – the work was back-breaking and the conditions poor, although the pay was relatively good for the gangs of migrant labourers who travelled round the country helping farmers with their harvests.

Markets seem to have a timeless quality about them. Maxwell Armfield drew this scene of the market place in Cambridge before the First World War, but it looks much the same today.

local record offices, although as records are largely working documents they may still be with the farms themselves.

OTHER RECORDS WHICH MIGHT BE OF USE

Census – identifies everybody in a village or farm and their occupations.
Deeds – can help to unravel the ownership of pieces of land.
Enclosure records – identifies land ownership at the time land was enclosed, normally in the latter half of the 18th century.
Maps – large scale maps will identify field patterns and field names, smaller scale maps will indicate the changing shape of villages as they grow or in some cases decline.
Newspapers – contain much about the day-to-day life of rural communities and the crises they faced.
Photographs – can reveal changing agricultural practices over a century or more, and give some idea of life in villages and farms. Many Victorian photographs seem curiously staged however, so the picture you are looking at may be one which the photographer has created rather than an accurate portrayal of rural life.
Oral history – memories of farm workers can tell you much about life and agricultural practices which have long disappeared.
Tithe records – compiled in the late 1830s and show land ownership and patterns towards the end of the agricultural revolution.

THEMES YOU MIGHT CONSIDER PURSUING

- What was grown or raised on local farms? Were there any crops unique to the area (such as hops)?
- In what ways did the physical nature of the area affect farming? What was the response to these natural conditions?
- Did what was grown change over time, perhaps as the response to outside events, such as the demands of war or a switch to market gardening to meet the demands of a rapidly expanding local town?
- Who owned the land? Was it a few large landowners or a number of small farmers? Did this change over time, and what were the implications for the crops grown?
- What about farming in urban areas? Many households kept pigs and chickens, and where possible people had gardens. Allotments develop from the 1890s and are little studied – why were they established and who worked on them?

A shopkeeper and his children stand proudly in front of their shop. From the newspaper advertisements the picture was taken during the Boer War, probably in a working class area, judging by the lurid articles promised. Since the Second World War we have lost tens of thousands of small local shops, as they were unable to compete against the supermarkets and chain stores. (photo courtesy: Mrs E. Robinson)

MARKETS AND SHOPS

Many towns grew up around markets and during the medieval period the right to hold a market was regarded as being precious, as it could lead to prosperity for the citizenry. Not every borough granted the right was successful – there could have been more established rivals nearby or the market was built in a place people could not easily get to.

The market place was often the centre of life in a town, attracting local farmers and merchants. In some towns, such as Boston and St Albans, market stalls became permanent shops, encroaching on the original market area. More often shops and inns grew up around the market place catering for the people who had come to buy and sell.

In many places a specially built market hall was erected as an expression of civic pride. During the 19th century local authorities built covered markets, usually in order to improve public health. They remain fascinating buildings to wander around.

Markets have been under severe pressure since the end of the Second World War, from competition from supermarkets and attempts by councils to redevelop town centres, although the lesson seems to have been learnt that markets add vitality to an area.

There have been shops since at least medieval times; although the recognisable shopfront with its large plate glass windows only slowly spread from London during the later half of the 18th century. The first multiple stores, with branches in a number of towns, was a development of the late Victorian period, as indeed was the department store. The post-war period however has seen the rapid growth of multiple stores, with the resultant loss of individual character which many shopping centres once possessed.

SECONDARY LITERATURE

The whole subject of markets and shops is a curiously neglected one – there is no current survey of the subject. The best place to start is the sections on market places and shops in Mark Girouard, *The English Town* (Yale University Press, 1990). A number of shops, such as Harrods and Selfridges and chain stores such as Sainsbury's and J. Lyons have had histories written about them. There are also some autobiographical accounts and diaries by shop owners, although naturally fewer from shop workers. These can be hard to track down.

MUSEUMS

A number of museums have recreated shops and indeed in a few cases whole streets. With the exception of the Robert Opie Collection of advertising in Gloucester, whose future is uncertain, there appears to be no museum dedicated to the subject.

ARCHIVES

The records of a number of shops can be found at local record offices and local studies libraries. They may include accounts, letter books, records of customers and orders taken from them, and perhaps more specialist items such as preparation books for chemists. The **National Register of Archives** should give you some idea of what survives where. There may also be deeds and other land records showing the changing property.

In addition, a number of chains and large shops maintain their own archives. Sainsbury's and Harrods are two institutions which do. From personal experience I have found them difficult to deal with as they are largely focused on helping the business rather than researchers, but it is unlikely that serious local historians will be turned away.

OTHER USEFUL SOURCES

Census – will enable you to pick out shop owners and shop workers. Most shop owners lived on the premises, so this may help you to plot where shops where. In addition a number of shops provided accommodation for unmarried shop workers and where this is the case this should be clearly shown.

Directories – shops will normally be listed in street and trade directories. These books should also give you a rough idea of when shops began and finished trading.

Newspapers – are an invaluable source. Where shops advertised, and by no means all saw the need to, the adverts offer a fascinating insight into what was being sold. Newspapers are also full of stories about shops and shopkeepers, such as the arrival of a new line or a robbery. Another useful source is trade papers such as *The Grocer* which will describe the changing fortunes of the trade.

Photographs – can show the changing nature of the shop frontage, although there are far fewer shots taken inside premises.

THEMES YOU MIGHT CONSIDER PURSUING

- A general history of retailing in your town.
- The history of the market.
- The history of a particular shop, or a particular row of shops.
- A study of why retailing prospered (or declined) in your area, perhaps taking a specific period – say the post-war period.
- An oral history of shop keepers and shop workers to discover how things have changed since they began working.

6
GETTING AROUND: TRAVEL AND TRANSPORT

●●●●●

The development of transport is largely the result of people's desire to travel ever faster and ever cheaper. It was not just individuals who sought speed, but farmers, industrialists and merchants as well who wanted to move goods as quickly as possible.

Before the 1750s travel was slow and cumbersome. If you wanted to get around you had three choices. The first was to walk, which was all that was open to the poor. The second was to use the horse or animal drawn vehicles to carry you where you wanted to go. And thirdly, you could take a boat to go from one port to another. Roads were generally poorly maintained, although the position changed as turnpike trusts improved stretches of road allowing people to use it in return for a small fee. By 1820 there were over a thousand such trusts which maintained 22,000 miles of road and charged tolls at 7,000 gates. With the onset of the railway, turnpikes lost much of their income as freight and people preferred faster and cheaper trains. During the Victorian period trusts were generally taken over by local government.

Although rivers had been carrying freight since medieval times, the amount was limited by the size of the waterway and the direction it flowed, which was not necessarily in the direction merchants and manufacturers wanted. The solution lay in building artificial waterways – the canals. Apart from a late sixteenth century example at Exeter, the first modern canal was built in 1760 around Manchester to carry coal. By the beginning of the 19th century the canal network was virtually complete, linking the industrial areas of the Midlands and the North with ports on the coast, particularly Liverpool and London.

The canal age, however, lasted barely seventy years. With the arrival of the railways they faded away, although freight continued to be

A busy day at the New Inn in Gloucester about 1800: This famous coaching inn still stands – a testament to the importance that such places had in the local economy. As well as looking after visitors, inns were often meeting places for local businessmen and magistrates.

carried until after the Second World War. Most were eventually taken over by their railway rivals. In 1948 they were nationalised and are now controlled by British Waterways. Since the 1960s canals have become an important leisure resource. Because of their intimate connection with the earliest days of the industrial revolution, a canal trip can often provide a fascinating insight into industrial development and, it has to be said, decay.

The first railways were horse-drawn and largely developed in collieries of the North East of England during the 18th century. The idea of using railways to carry passengers rather than freight was slower to catch on, although the first passenger service was probably on the horse-drawn railway between Swansea and Mumbles in 1807. But it was not until the instant success of the line between Liverpool and Manchester, that the railway rapidly spread outside the industrial heartlands. Within twenty years the network had largely been completed.

The railway station at York is a memorable introduction to an ancient city. Even after a hundred and fifty years the audacity of its architecture takes the breath away. Such monuments to the railway age reinforce the status that the iron rail had during the Victorian period.

The railway had an impact on society which no form of transport before or indeed afterwards had. For the first time it was possible for people, of all classes, to travel great distances in relative comfort. The size of the network allowed freight, such as agricultural produce or industrial goods, to be conveyed easily from the producer to where it was needed. Railway lines transformed the look of the countryside, while in towns stations, marshalling yards and viaducts had a major impact on the built environment. Indeed, the power of the railway was so great that it led to the building of new towns and villages to house the people it employed, or the development of others to cater for the new needs created by the iron road.

The railway age itself lasted barely a century. The railways were nationalised in 1948 largely because they were bankrupt. Despite the veneer of prosperity the inter-war years had not been good ones for the railways. During the 1920s and 1930s the 'Big Four' companies faced increasing competition again from roads in the form of cars, buses and lorries, which were cheaper and could reach places that the railway never could.

Since the Second World War car usage has both changed the physical appearance of urban areas, with motorways and by-passes, and enhanced people's mobility, with the resulting decline of traditional markets and shopping centres replaced by car-friendly new towns (such as Stevenage and Milton Keynes), supermarkets and shopping precincts.

It goes without saying that transport has had a major impact on the landscape and the townscape. A lot of these changes can be followed on the ground or by a close study of Ordnance Survey or other maps. Things to look out for include:

- Unusual twists and turns on roads, such as unnecessary curves which might indicate ancient estate boundaries or the wish to pass around a building which has long since been demolished.
- Unusually straight or wide roads in towns may mean that the road has been improved by widening and straightening at some time. In the country straightness may indicate a Roman road (this is usually marked on OS maps), a greenway or drovers track along which cattle might have been driven to market.
- You can usually tell roads built as the result of enclosure in the 18th century, by their width, straightness, and by the wide margin between the road and neighbouring fields.
- Road names may indicate former uses. In towns, for example, a Station Road without a station in it is a sure sign that once upon a time it led to a railway station which has since disappeared. In the country, roads or tracks called Salt Way may indicate an old pedlars' track upon which salt was transported across the country.
- Canals and rivers often quite clearly display former uses. Canals in particular have towpaths next to the waterway, so it is usually fairly easy to walk up and down them. You might come across old bollards to which boats were moored, or small docks, which allowed boats to be loaded with goods. Locks and neighbouring lock keeper's cottages are also often of some architectural interest.
- Occasionally there may be mills, factories or houses near the canal built to take advantage of the new canal's facilities.
- Railways of course had a major impact on town- and landscape. Even though the railway may have long gone, there could still be warehouses, viaducts, bridges, cuttings and even forlorn-looking former railway stations. It should also be possible to trace former lines on OS maps as they are usually marked.

By the end of the nineteenth century, the more scenic canals and rivers had become popular with holidaymakers, as readers of Jerome K. Jerome's Three Men in a Boat *will remember. This is a bustling day at Boulter's Lock on the Thames near Maidenhead.*

- Early railway companies often spent large sums on railway stations and these can be of particular architectural merit. Indeed, a number of stations are worth more than a cursory glance as they may contain evidence of the heyday of railway travel and the Victorian class system, with third class and lady's waiting rooms.
- Again, in most towns, there is likely to be housing built for railway workers or for other people attracted to the area by the new transport links.
- The presence of modern by-passes and motorways as well as widened roads is sadly too all obvious. Occasionally you may find short stretches of roads which for one reason or another were never completed or fully widened. It may also be an interesting exercise to try to reconstruct the street pattern of what disappeared under concrete.

THEMES YOU MIGHT CONSIDER PURSUING

- The history of a particular transport facility in your area – how it came to be there, how it developed and changed over time. If it has closed you might want to look at the impact on the local community. This could involve, say, a study of a canal or even something as contemporary as an airport. There seems, for example, to be very little research on the development and impact of roads locally. General sources for studies like this, might include: **local government records, newspapers, oral history, old photographs** and **maps**. It is always worth looking to see whether there is already a history of aspects of transport, perhaps written from the perspective of an enthusiast (for example on a particular railway branch line), which can be consulted.
- The impact of transport on a town or district. This may be very difficult to measure, but its convenient location may have seen the growth of coaching inns, the arrival of the railway may have led to an expansion in economic activity, or more recently the building of a by-pass may have seen the decline of a town centre as retailers opened out-of-town stores. General sources for studies like this include: **local government records, newspapers, census, oral history, old photographs** and **maps**.
- Who was employed locally in transport related work. Were they in the main local people, or perhaps migrants with skills or attracted by high wages? Occasionally you may find company staff registers or wage books, or perhaps memoirs, but you are likely to have to rely on the **census, newspapers** and, maybe, **oral history** as general sources.

RECORDS AND SOURCES

Roads were maintained by the local **parish**, although the work was increasingly directed by **quarter sessions** and, after 1888, by **county councils**. A rate was levied on the richer householders to pay for this work, which was often carried out by paupers and other poor residents. The supervision of this work was entrusted to an unpaid surveyor of the highway, appointed annually by justices of the peace. As this office could entail considerable work and little reward, it consequently was not a popular position to have. As a result roads, particularly the main highways, tended to be poorly looked after. Such money as was spent

Eighteenth century travellers constantly grumbled about the state of the highway, although matters improved considerably with the construction of macadamised turnpike roads. Rural parishes employed paupers to maintain local roads, although urban vestries usually employed people, as here, to keep the streets in a reasonable condition.

by the parish was likely to go on maintaining local roads, which were the ones most often used by the ratepayers.

What improved matters was the introduction, from the beginning of the 18th century, of turnpiked roads operated by private trusts licensed by Parliament. For a small fee or toll people could travel on properly maintained roads. As a result journey times were shortened. The fate of turnpikes was sealed with the arrival of the railways in the 1830s. Income from tolls fell as travellers preferred to go by train. Most eventually were dissolved and their duties taken over by local councils.

Records relating to roads are overwhelmingly at local record offices, where they may be found in various places. **Parish records** may well include accounts prepared by the surveyor of the highway and **vestry** minutes about the maintenance and construction of local roads.

Quarter sessions records may include material relating to the maintenance of local roads and structures such as bridges. You may also find the surviving records of turnpike trusts here, as their work was often taken over by the Sessions when the companies went out of business from the 1840s onwards.

Local record offices might also have records of local **improvement commissioners** who were appointed by special act of parliament, usually to improve sanitary conditions locally. Roads were often included amongst their duties.

After 1889, with the creation of county and county borough councils, responsibility for the maintenance of roads passed to these new authorities. There was almost always a highways committee which was responsible for roads and whose minutes and other papers may be available. There may also be material on later road building and widening schemes, although for larger ventures the Ministry of Transport in London may also have been involved, so there could also be records at the **Public Record Office** (PRO).

The PRO, however, is most often used by local historians looking at the records of the canal and record companies which passed to the Office in the 1970s. These archives had been taken over by the British Transport Commission after nationalisation in 1948. The contents vary considerably between individual companies – the most complete are for the Great Western Railway. The PRO also has the records of British Rail between 1948 and the early 1970s. This material is easy to use for two reasons – it is sorted by company and there is a comprehensive card index arranged by subject. The best guide is Cliff Edwards, *Railway Records at the Public Record Office* (PRO, 2001).

The National Railway Museum, Leeman Rd, York YO26 4XJ (*www.nrm.org.uk*) also has sizeable holdings. The completeness of these records varies greatly, but there may be company minutes or files of correspondence about building new railway stations, maps showing the route lines were to take, or ephemera such as photographs or posters advertising new services.

As canals and railways could only be built after an Act of Parliament had been obtained, the **House of Lords Record Office** may well have minutes of investigating committees, petitions and records of debates about the construction of these facilities. Similar records should exist for acts instituting improvement commissioners.

Local record offices and local studies libraries may have material, photographs or press cuttings about, for example, new stations or closure of branch lines. Official records may be harder to come by, but there could be mention in vestry or council minute books of the sale of land to railway companies or of permission to build a new station.

Appendix I
GLOSSARY

•••••

This appendix describes many types of documents referred to elsewhere in the book and the use that might be made of them by local historians. Also included are definitions of some common terms, which appear in the text, or which you may come across elsewhere. A much more comprehensive dictionary for local historians is the *Oxford Companion to Local and Family History*. Another useful, if slightly dated, guide is John Richardson, *The Local Historian's Encyclopaedia* (Historical Publications, 1986).

ADMINISTRATIVE STRUCTURE

The structure of most administrative bodies has changed little over the centuries. Decisions are made in committee or council, either a central body, sometimes called an executive committee. For larger bodies permanent sub-committees, or temporary ones considering certain issues, may be appointed. They will usually report to the central committee in order that their decisions or recommendations are ratified. Decisions are normally recorded in minute books, which may also record something of the discussion which took place at meetings. Because of their importance these books often survive. Other records which may also be in existence include: accounts, committee papers, published annual reports, lists of members, and miscellaneous reports.

AGRICULTURAL REVOLUTION

The Agricultural Revolution occurred at roughly the same time as the industrial revolution. It was largely the result of new methods of farming which increased productivity substantially, together with new machinery, which cut the need for labour. Displaced agricultural workers drifted towards the new industrial areas or emigrated to America or the British colonies. One sign of the changes was the **enclosure** of land. This happened roughly between 1760 and 1830, beginning in the Midlands. The resulting enclosure maps and apportionment documents clearly show who owned what land and the field patterns. Incomplete sets of these maps are at the Public Record Office and county record offices. A good introduction to the subject is J.D. Chambers and G.E. Mingay, *The Agricultural Revolution, 1750-1880* (Batsford, 1966).

ARCHIVES

An archive (or record office) is where original documents of an historic nature are stored and made available to researchers. There are at least a thousand such archives in Britain, varying in size from the Public Record Office, which has over a million records in its care and tens of thousands of visitors each year, down to small numbers of historic records kept by a school, business, or charity. For more about this archival network see the chapter on Getting Started in Local History.

BOROUGHS

Medieval boroughs were distinguished from other towns by the charters granted to them by the king, which generally related to the privileges of holding markets, the ability of corporations to govern the borough, and the election of members of parliament. By the late 18th century the system had largely fallen into decay; many boroughs were little more than villages, while growing industrial towns had no effective means of local government. During the 19th century many reforms were made, particularly the 1832 Reform Act which stopped the smallest and most unrepresentative boroughs (known as rotten boroughs) from electing MPs, while borough status was granted to many large towns. The 1888 Local Government Act clearly defined the responsibilities of boroughs and created fifty or so county boroughs which had the powers of county councils. This two-tier system was abolished in 1974 and most boroughs were absorbed into district councils.

Most borough records should be at county record offices. A few places, including Coventry, Hull, Portsmouth, Southampton and York have their own archives. For more about the records created by boroughs see John West, *Town Records* (Phillimore, 1983).

BUSINESS RECORDS

Finding records of specific companies can be very difficult: entrepreneurs usually have other things on their mind than preserving old records. The records mostly likely to have survived are minutes and papers relating to the ownership of the company. Some firms, such as breweries, have collections of ephemera such as posters, brochures and other advertising material.

The **National Register of Archives** should be able to tell you which company's records are held where. They have produced several excellent free leaflets on company records. Large collections of business archives are at the Guildhall Library (mainly for those in the City of London), the Modern Records Centre at the University of Warwick, and at the University of Glasgow (such as the Scottish Brewing Archive).

The Business Archives Council, 101 Whitechapel High Street, London E1 7RE (*www.gla.ac.uk/bac*) may also be able to help. Over the years the Council has published guides to the records of a number of industries including chemicals and brewing, copies of which may be at reference or university libraries.

If the company you are interested in was a limited company, they had to register at Companies House, Crown Way, Maindy, Cardiff CF4 3UZ (*www.companies-house.gov.uk*) and submit financial returns and details of share holdings. Older records are now at the **Public Record Office** (PRO), although they will only tell you about shareholdings and shareholders, and when the company was formed and when it was wound up.

The PRO also has some bankruptcy records; these go back to the 18th century and may contain a lot of material you can't find elsewhere. Details of bankruptcies were published in the *London Gazette*, copies of which can be consulted at large reference libraries. The PRO also has a complete set. There is also a comprehensive free leaflet (no 54) on *Registration of Companies and Businesses*, which can be downloaded from the PRO website.

Although they are public records, colliery company records and those of the National Coal Board have been deposited in local record offices. Most railway and canal company records (including British

Rail and the British Transport Commission) are also at the PRO. Again local record offices may also have certain records relating to local railway companies.

If the company is still operating it may be worth approaching them. Large companies often have an archivist or records manager who is usually very willing to help, provided you don't ask too much of them. Remember that large companies often absorbed many smaller companies whose records they may still have. The big brewers, such as Bass and Whitbread, for example, absorbed many dozens of small local brewers whose records are often in the company archives.

CALENDARS

Published transcriptions (and where necessary translations) of records, usually from the medieval and Tudor and Stuart periods. Both the PRO and county record societies have published many such calendars.

CENSUS

Census returns offer a chance of historical voyeurism, providing a snapshot of Victorian communities on one night, normally in early April every ten years. This information is nearly impossible to find elsewhere. The records list almost everybody, household by household, giving details such as age, occupation and place of birth. From them one can work out some idea of the economic and demographic structure, answering questions such as where did migrants come from? What was the size of the family? Who employed servants?

The first British census was taken in 1801 with the aim of discovering whether the population was growing or declining. Subsequently censuses have been taken every ten years. The first census however for which individual returns survive is 1841, although more information can be gleaned from the 1851 and subsequent censuses. The last census presently available is for 1891. The 1901 census will be opened in January 2002 and will, for the first time, be available on the internet at *www.census.pro.gov.uk* although a fee will be charged. The best introduction to using these records for local historians is Edward Higgs, *A Clearer Sense of the Census: Victorian Censuses and Historical Research* (HMSO, 1996). There are also a number of books about the census written with the family historian in mind.

For studies of 19th century towns or industries census records are an invaluable source, for they contain information about individuals which is unobtainable elsewhere. Here at Sandringham in 1891, the Prince of Wales is enumerated next to a parlourmaid.

A complete set of census returns, together with street indexes and surname indexes, is at the **Family Records Centre**. Most county record offices and local studies libraries have sets for their area. Censuses are only available on microfilm which can be difficult to read at times. The 1881 census, however, has been produced on searchable CD-ROM.

The raw material, contained in census enumerators' books (CEBs), was sent to London for analysis. The results were published in a series of **Parliamentary Papers** which contain useful material, although published analyses, for the 19th century at least, tend to be at county or city level, rather than by village or town.

COUNTY AND LOCAL RECORD OFFICES

All English (and most Welsh) counties, and a few cities have a record office, which collects material for their area. They are described in more detail in chapter 2.

COUNTY COUNCILS

County councils were first elected in 1889. They took over the local government responsibilities of quarter sessions, including the maintenance of roads, some housing and planning duties, and (from 1902) education. Their records are little used by local historians, which is a pity because they can be very informative.

Most councillors initially came from the local gentry, although this gradually declined during the 20th century. As a result the political representation on councils tended to be either Conservative or independent (which in practice usually was much the same thing). The first Labour run councils in Durham and Monmouthshire were elected in 1919.

Records of county councils should be with the county records office, although those for the 1970s and later may not have yet been transferred.

DEEDS, ESTATE AND PROPERTY RECORDS

Title deeds, indentures and the like for particular properties can go back centuries, listing both the purchaser and the seller together with details of the land or property being sold. These records are usually well indexed and once you have grasped how they are laid out are easy to use. Most local record offices have large collections of this material. They are useful in tracing the ownership of houses and land, working out its value at a particular time, and changing boundaries as parcels of land were bought and sold. A useful introduction to the records is A.D. Carr 'Deeds of Title' in K.M. Thompson, *Short Guides to Records: First Series – Guides 1-24* (Historical Association, 1994).

There were two county-wide deeds registries, for Middlesex (now at the Greater London Record Office, 40 Northampton Road, London EC1R 0HB) and for the West Riding of Yorkshire (West Yorkshire Archive Service, Registry of Deeds, Newstead Rd, Wakefield WF1 2DE) where, as the name suggests, deeds were registered and kept together, so it is relatively easy to trace the ownership of a house or piece of land.

DEMOGRAPHY

The study of population. For local historians this may mean examining the growth (or, indeed, decline) of population in a particular town or parish. Good introductions to the subject include Peter Laslett, *The World We Have Lost: Further Explored* (Methuen, 1983), E.A Wrigely, *Introduction to English Historical Demography* (1966), and E.A. Wrigely and R.S. Schofield, *The Population History of England: a Reconstruction* (1981). The major sources for studies of this kind have been the **census** and **parish records**. The Local Population Studies Society, 78 Harlow Crescent, Harrogate, HG2 0PN is worth joining if you are interested in the subject. See also chapter 3.

DIRECTORIES

Trade and court directories begin in the late eighteenth century, but are most useful for the period between 1850 and 1914. There are several types of directory, the most important of which is the general trade directory. This is usually arranged with a trade section with the names of persons engaged in each trade, an alphabetical list of people

Old directories can be used to work out which trades took place where in a town. This page comes from a directory of Kew in Surrey published in 1900.

together with their occupations, and a classified alphabetical arrangement of streets, containing the names and occupations of householders. The other major type of directory was the court directory which usually lists people regarded as being in 'society' locally – a very partial view of town life.

Directories list all the trades and occupations in a town. It is thus a very simple task to work out which trades were based where. Over the years you can trace the growth and changes in local industry so it is possible to discover roughly when companies started or ceased trading.

Libraries and local archives may have sets for their areas. The best national collection is at the Guildhall Library, Aldermanbury, London EC2P 2EJ (telephone: 020 7606 3030). A list of directories can be found in Gareth Shaw and Alison Tipper, *British Directories: A Bibliography and Guide to Directories Published in England and Wales, 1850-1950* (Leicester University Press, 1988).

There are also professional directories which can provide useful information. *Crockford's*, for example, lists all Church of England clergy. They can however be difficult to track down, although reference libraries and the **Society of Genealogists** should have sets of some of the more common. Another related source are town guides published by local councils to promote their towns. These guides may list local companies, as least those who paid to be included, and give a rosy view of the area's industries and prospects. Local studies libraries often have copies of guides, which may go back to before the First World War.

DOMESDAY BOOK

One of my biggest thrills while working at the Public Record Office was the chance to touch the Domesday Book. When they were rebinding the book in 1986, staff had the opportunity to handle it under strictly controlled circumstances. I also remember the day I ordered it up by mistake, but we won't go into that.

The Domesday Book is perhaps the most important English document. It was commissioned by William the Conqueror in 1085 to discover who owned what in England and how much this land was worth. It covered everywhere in England apart from the northern extremities of England and the cities of London, Tamworth and Winchester. The Book received its name from comparisons with the

Domesday, the Last Day of Judgment.

The original is at the **Public Record Office**, where it is on display in the Visitor and Education Centre. Fortunately the content has been published in various editions, the most highly regarded of which is the Phillimore county edition. Phillimore has recently published it in a fully-indexed form on CD-ROM.

Although it is full of invaluable information it is difficult to interpret and full of pitfalls for the unwary. For the amateur historian however it gives a tantalising glimpse into the economic life of a village nine hundred years ago, with details of who owned property before and after the Norman Conquest, whether there was a mill, and numbers of livestock which the village supported.

There are a number of books about the Domesday Book. One of the best is Elizabeth M. Hallam, *Domesday through Nine Centuries* (Thames and Hudson, 1986).

ENCLOSURE

The extinguishing of common rights over common land, open fields and waste fields by agreement of local landowners. The process started in the late medieval period, but reached its peak in the half century after 1750 when thousands of private Acts of Parliament were passed authorising local commissioners to enclose these lands. The process had virtually finished by 1850.

Copies of enclosure acts should be with either the local record office or the House of Lords Record Office. A set of enclosure maps and accompanying documents is at the Public Record Office. A good book on the subject is Steven Hollowell, *Enclosure Records for Historians* (Phillimore, 2000), although a simple introduction can be found in L.M. Munby, *Short Guides to Records: First Series* (Historical Association, 1994).

EVIDENCE

All historical research is a process of gathering evidence and making a judgment about what happened. Evidence may come in many forms, such as documents found at an archive, the physical remains on the ground, or interviews with elderly residents on a particular topic. This evidence can however be incomplete (vital documents may be missing), biased (a newspaper report pandering to the prejudices of its readers) or just plain wrong (an interviewee thinking they were present at an event, when they weren't). Ideally all evidence should be cross-checked with other sources for accuracy, so that a reasonably truthful picture of what happened emerges. Unfortunately it is not always possible to do this.

FIELDWORK

A term sometimes used to refer to the process of physically seeing what evidence the landscape or townscape can offer to illustrate its history.

GREY LITERATURE

A term sometimes used to describe ephemeral printed material, such as newspapers, pamphlets or posters, which is original but several copies of which may exist in various places.

HUNDREDS

Old sub-divisions of counties. In some areas they were called wapentakes, rapes or ridings.

IMPROVEMENT COMMISSIONERS

During the last half of the eighteenth and the first half of the nineteenth century, concerned local citizens could obtain private Acts of Parliament to set up 'improvement' or 'street' commissioners to improve conditions in towns. Although their powers varied greatly, they usually had responsibility for rebuilding and clearing streets, public health and sanitation, and sometimes housing. Their records are usually at local record offices.

INDUSTRIAL ARCHAEOLOGY

The study of industrial sites, machinery and buildings. It grew out of concern in the 1960s and 1970s that Britain's industrial heritage was being lost, and much time even now is spent recording sites and finding alternative uses for redundant buildings. The major organisation in the field is the Association for Industrial Archaeology which issues an excellent journal, and organises conferences and seminars. It can be contacted at AIA Office, School of Archaeological Studies, University of Leicester, Leicester LE1 7RH (*www.industrial-archaeology.org.uk*).

The best introduction to the subject is Michael Stratton and Barrie Trinder, *Industrial England* (Batsford, 1997). Also of interest is Barrie Trinder, *The Making of the Industrial Landscape* (Dent, 1982), and Michael Stratton and Barrie Trinder, *Twentieth Century Industrial Archaeology* (Spon Press, 2000).

INDUSTRIAL REVOLUTION

An industrial revolution is the process by which an economy is changed from being primarily agricultural to one which is dominated by manufacturing. The industrial revolution in England and Wales began about 1750 and lasted roughly a century, although some argue that it is still continuing. Why the first industrial revolution occurred in Britain, has often been debated by historians. There seems to have been no one cause, but a variety of factors including new technologies, ample supplies of coal and iron, a flexible banking system and individuals who were willing to invest in new enterprises, and a liberal and relatively open society which encouraged innovation.

For the local historian, the industrial revolution marks the change between a rural, stable and hierarchical society and the world with which we are familiar today. It was however a gradual change. The evidence for this transformation can still be seen in the buildings and artefacts left behind, from canals to derelict mills. The records also demonstrate the upheaval, from new enterprises such as the railways to the attempts to deal with the unemployed and poorly housed.

There are a number of books on the industrial revolution, including E.J. Hobsbawm, *Industry and Empire* (Penguin, 1969), and Peter Mathias, *The First Industrial Nation* (Cambridge University Press, 1969).

JUSTICES OF THE PEACE

The first justices of the peace (JPs), sometimes called magistrates, were appointed in the 13th century. Their powers grew considerably during the Tudor period. They were (and are) appointed by the sovereign, usually on the advice of the Lord Lieutenant or other prominent local landowners. Until the twentieth century they were largely made up of local gentry and other prominent men. They had a dual responsibility for administering the county (until 1888) and dispensing justice in petty cases. This dual responsibility is shown in the records, which are usually held at county record offices.

LOCAL GOVERNMENT (AND PARISH RECORDS)

No study of a local community should be complete without using local official records. The decisions of local councils and related bodies had a profound impact on local people and the areas they lived in. This impact is little studied by local historians. Local government has a reputation for being boring, and councillors for either being bores or corrupt. Neither is true, although it has to be admitted local government finance is pretty tedious!

Before the late 1880s local government was split between parishes, town, city or borough councils and quarter sessions. **Parishes** had the responsibility for helping the poor before 1834, maintaining the highway, as well as running the local Anglican church. For more about these records see W.E. Tate, *The Parish Chest* (3rd edition, Phillimore, 1983).

Magistrates sitting in **Quarter Sessions** had a mixture of duties, the most important of which was to act as a court. But they also had a miscellany of other duties from supervising local freemasons and friendly societies to registering alehouses and gamekeepers, and running local prisons. These records are listed in Jeremy Gibson, *Quarter Sessions for Family Historians: A Select List* (4th edition, Federation of Family History Societies, 1995). Several other 'Gibson Guides' cover aspects of records kept by the Quarter Sessions.

Towns and **boroughs** had more powers, regulated in the cases of boroughs by jealously guarded charters received from the Crown. These charters often granted the borough a weekly market, if the town was to thrive. Borough corporations and town councils were revived during the 19th century with new powers to tackle public health and new councillors with ideas of civic pride. For more about these bodies and their records see Stephen Porter, *Exploring Urban History: Sources for Local Historians* (Batsford, 1990) and John West, *Town Records* (Phillimore, 1983).

The nineteenth century also saw the growth of semi-autonomous local bodies responsible for specific duties such as the Poor Law, sewers and water supply (generally known as Improvement Commissions), and education.

The establishment of county councils and the patchwork of boroughs, that were set up in 1889 (and urban and rural districts formed in 1894) disrupted the old order by giving carefully regulated powers to the various tiers. There is no up to date history of local government in the 20th century let alone an account of the records themselves, although local record offices may have leaflets or guides which explain their holdings.

The records most likely to survive are minute books for the council, or other body, and its constituent committees. From the 1890s they were often printed up with useful indexes, although they may not be terribly informative. There may also be accounts, either manuscript lists prepared by churchwardens detailing what a parish spent on poor relief or maintaining the highway or printed accounts of a council's spending. If you are interested in the recent history of an area it is worth seeing whether there are any district plans prepared during and immediately after the Second World War which offer a vision (all too rarely fulfilled) of a better post-war world.

As with all records, the survival rate is patchy. The City of London never seems to have thrown anything away, but in the smaller boroughs very little may have been kept. Decisions are recorded in council committee minutes normally found at county record offices, but whether the accompanying papers and correspondence survive is chancy. Correspondence with central government may be at the **Public Record Office**. More modern records may be closed or otherwise unavailable. Unlike central government, where historic records have to be produced for public access after 30 years, there is no such commitment in local government, so you may have difficulty gaining access to material not transferred to the record office.

The records are useful for almost every aspect of local history research whether it be assigning street names and numbers when rebuilding bomb-damaged districts after the Second World War, to educational policy and the appointment of teachers, or the administration of the poor law and the clearance of slums.

MAPS

Old maps are a valuable source for the local historian, especially in towns where changes were relatively rapid. You can check the growth of urban areas – and even, on the largest scale maps, the location of lamp posts – or changing field boundaries.

Ordnance Survey (OS) maps are the best known and most important. They begin in the early 19th century. For rural areas the small-scale one inch or two and a half inch to the mile series (now the Landranger 1:50,000 and Explorer 1:25,000 series) are probably the most useful. Modern OS maps are widely available from bookshops or direct from the Survey themselves. There is also have an interesting web site (*www.ordnancesurvey.gov.uk*). They publish a variety of large-scale maps showing the townscape in some detail, the best known of which are the six-inch and twenty-five inch series, although some scales were as large as one to five hundred feet.

The most complete set of Ordnance Survey maps, including sketches and rough drawings, is at the **British Library**. The **Public Record Office** (PRO) also has a pretty good collection. Local record offices should have sets for their areas.

David and Charles have reprinted the first series of one-inch maps. They give a picture of the English (and Welsh) countryside as the railways arrived, although the quality of reproduction is not always high. Alan Godfrey has reproduced large-scale maps of many English towns. Most reference libraries or record offices sell such maps for their area or you can buy them from him directly at Alan Godfrey Maps, Prospect Business Park, Leadgate, Consett, Co. Durham, DH8 7PW (*www.alangodfreymaps.co.uk*). It is also possible to download extracts from old maps on the internet at *www.old-maps.co.uk2* and buy copies (which are rather more expensive than Alan Godfrey's).

A concise introduction to OS maps can be found in Richard Oliver, 'Ordnance Survey Maps' in K.M. Thompson, *Short Guides to Records: Second Series – Guides 25-48* (Historical Association, 1997). More detailed information is in Richard Oliver's *Ordnance Survey Maps – A Concise Guide for Historians* (Charles Close Society, 1993), which contains a wealth of information about the OS and its development with special emphasis on the maps most useful for historians.

Ordnance Survey maps are of course not the only ones available to the local historian. The earliest maps date from the 15th century, although they can be difficult to use. The 18th century saw the development of modern mapping, particularly for military use, hence the Ordnance Survey. Of course, over time maps have been drawn up for any number of purposes from plotting where bombs landed during the Blitz to road layouts. My favourites are the maps that accompany Booth's Survey of London, conducted in the 1880s, which show the social class of the inhabitants street by street in Inner London: a great conversation piece even today!

The most important of the pre-Ordnance Survey maps are enclosure maps which were drawn up, parish by parish, to show land enclosed. Similar, in some ways, are the detailed tithe maps that show land ownership and the lay-out of fields drawn up under the Tithe Commutation Act, 1836. A nearly complete set of maps with accompanying schedules showing who owned what is at the PRO. Many record offices also have sets for their areas. More about both series of maps is included in L.M. Munby, *Short Guide to Records: First Series – Guides 1-24* (Historical Association, 1994), and other introductory books to local history also cover the records in some detail.

Both **enclosure** and tithe maps are relatively well known tools for the local historian. What remains little known are the Valuation Office maps and books. The government conducted a survey, between 1910 and 1916, which tried to ascertain the value of every property in England and Wales. The maps are based on large scale Ordnance Survey plans of the period, while the books contain a description of every house and the facilities it had. Both maps and plans are at the PRO, and leaflets are available explaining how to use these sometimes tricky records. They are described in more detail in William Foot, *Maps for Family History* (PRO Publications, 1994).

If you are interested in urban areas, fire insurance maps show the landownership and boundaries of individual buildings, together with an indication of a building's height and whether there was a basement. Copies of these very colourful maps are usually with local record offices or local studies libraries. They are described in more detail in Peter A. Neaverson, 'Fire Insurance Plans' in K.M. Thompson, *Short Guides to Records: Second Series – Guides 25-48* (Historical Association, 1997).

A simple introduction to maps can be found in Philip Riden, *Local History: A Handbook for Beginners* (Merton Priory Press, 1998). A more detailed guide is Brian Paul Hindle, *Maps for Local Historians* (Batsford, 1988).

MONEY

Until February 1971, a pound sterling consisted of 20 shillings (abbreviated as s). Each shilling was made up of 12 pennies (d). In turn pennies were divided into 4 farthings. You may occasionally come across mention of guineas (21s), marks (6s 8d), crowns (5s) and groats (4d).

It is almost impossible to make a comparison between what a pound was worth in the past and what it is worth now. In Tudor times a pound would have bought goods valued between £200 and £500 today, but almost everything was proportionally more expensive then. A book cost about 5s in 1600: 400 years later using this multiplier, it would cost between £50 and £125. However, you can buy a new hardback book for less than £20. Outside the upper classes, people were paid proportionally much less than today. An agricultural labourer, for example, might receive no more than £10 a year. Today's agricultural labourers are still poorly paid, but they can afford to buy books. For such a labourer to have spent a week's wages on a book in 1600 would have been unthinkable.

The best introduction to the subject is: Lionel Munby, *How Much is that Worth?* (British Association for Local History, 1996).

NEWSPAPERS AND MAGAZINES

Newspapers can be a very important source for local historians. If nothing else it is possible to pick up a good impression of what it was like to live during the period. The adverts of course are always amusing. I'm not sure however you should base a local history book on material solely from newspapers, as they only offer one view of the period, a view coloured by the usually conservative convictions of the editor or owner.

Most papers were established in the mid-Victorian period, after stamp duty was repealed. For the first time ordinary people could afford to buy newspapers. As a result there was an explosion in titles published. The heyday of the local newspaper was the period between 1880 and 1970 when most events were covered in great detail.

There are problems, however, in using newspapers – particularly the vast amount of information to be found in each issue. Few papers, with the exception of *The Times*, are indexed. This means that researchers must have a reasonable idea of when the event they are interested in took place. To a certain extent this might be overcome if the reference or local studies library has a collection of press cuttings. Many of these collections go back before the First World War and are extensively indexed. Indexes to *The Times* have been published on CD and sets sometimes can be found in reference and university libraries. The PRO Library also has a copy of the index between 1784 and 1905.

The British Library Newspaper Library holds the biggest collection of newspapers in the country. The Library's catalogue is now on-line (*www.bl.uk*) so it is fairly easy to see which newspapers were published for your area: you may be surprised at the variety, although most existed for only a few years. The catalogue also includes trade papers and journals which are very useful if you are studying a particular trade or profession, such as breweries or cotton factories. A list of provincial papers can also be found in Jeremy Gibson, *Local Newspapers 1750-1920: A Select Location List* (Federation of Family History Societies, 1989).

Local studies libraries or local record offices should have papers, usually on microfilm, for their area. The Newsplan programme, supported by lottery money, hopes to produce a catalogue of this material as well as to microfilm and conserve newspapers where appropriate.

Another underused source for local historians is magazines. With the advent of mass literacy and cheap printing from the 1880s onwards there was a surge of magazines produced by churches, companies, clubs and societies. If they survive (and this can be a big if) they can offer a fascinating, if often over-written, account of an institution's development and activities. In addition many bodies, such as charities and clubs, published an annual report summarising the year's activities with the accounts. Also of interest are trade magazines and journals, particularly if you are studying a particular industry. Again, the British Library Newspaper Library, local record offices and local studies libraries are obvious places to start. The **Public Record Office** has sets of railway company magazines.

ORAL HISTORY

Oral history is spoken history, the recording of people's memories and stories. Over the past 30 years listening to people has emerged as a means of providing new information about areas of local history not covered by printed or manuscript sources. There are a number of books on the practical aspects of oral history – one of the best is Stephen Caunce, *Oral History for Local Historians* (Longman, 1994). The National Sound Archive, based at the British Library, holds the largest collection of such tapes. Their catalogue, together with samples from their holdings, can now be searched at the Library's web site (*www.bl.uk*).

PARLIAMENTARY PAPERS

Parliamentary Papers, sometimes called Blue Books, are another passion of mine. They too are a source often overlooked by local historians. As the name suggests this is material, such as minutes of committees, reports, and financial accounts, ordered by Parliament (normally the House of Commons) to be printed. Larger university and reference libraries may have sets, and the PRO has a copy on microfiche in the Microfilm Reading Room. Detailed indexes exist between the late 18th century and 1949, which are now available on CD at the PRO and in larger reference and university libraries. There is no modern introduction to these papers, but readers might find Maurice Bond, *The Records of Parliament: A Guide for Genealogists and Local Historians* (Phillimore, 1964) useful.

They offer a wealth of information, much of which is not obtainable elsewhere. Annual reports of the Poor Law Commissioners, and its successors, contain a lot of correspondence with and about local boards of guardians on a variety of topics. It is thus possible to trace the development of friendly societies, town by town, over nearly a century, from returns of societies made between 1828 and 1910. This is not possible from material in local record offices. From verbatim minutes of various select committees' enquiries into industrial and agricultural conditions one can build up a picture of what it was like working in individual trades during the industrial revolution.

PARISH

The parish was the basic unit of local government until 1888. Before then rural parishes, in particular, had both an ecclesiastical role as the centre for Anglican worship, and through the Vestry to administer poor relief (before 1834), maintain the highway and keep the peace. Family historians will be familiar with the parish registers of baptisms, marriages, and burials, but local record offices may also hold

1624	Nov.	20	Joane "adultera." dau. of Susan Mihill.
	Dec.	2	John son of Nicholas Deckham.
		26	Jane dau. of John Wattkins.
		30	John son of Thomas Acton.
1624-5	Jan.	13	Helena dau. of Walter Griffen.
		16	"Chistofer son" of Renall Ashen.
		„	Elizabeth dau. of Tho. Higgs.
		30	John son of Richard Tuck.
	Feb.	3	Douglas dau. [sic] of Mr John Garret.
		9	Robert son of Robert Hall.
		13	Martha dau. of Tho. Redriffe.
		18	Henry son of Samuell Chambers.
	Mch.	3	Phanuell son of Robert Bourne.
		6	Michaell son of Michaell Fuellin.
		10	Robert son of Robert Trotter.
		13	Elizabeth dau. of William Snowe.
		19	Mary dau. of Thomas Curtes.
1625	Apl.	10	Audrie dau. of Thomas Kindar.
		24	John son of Caleb Dalton.
	May	1	William son of Will. Greeneland.
		8	Richard son of Will. Greene, junior.
		„	Will. Evans son of Ryce Evans, a travailing stranger whose wife laye in at Sheene.
		15	Henry son of Will. Hill of Kew.
		„	Hanna dau. of Roger Veasie.
		26	Percivall son (spurius) of Mary Browne.
	June	12	Joane dau. of Walter Hayes.
		22	Elizabeth dau. of John Mercer.
		26	Robert son of Henry Hyett.
	July	14	Marie dau. of James Rosse.
	Aug.	7	John son of Anthoney Sugar.
		10	Susan dau. of Will. King of St Bride's Parish.
		„	John and Anne childⁿ of one Thomas Ayers, a Stranger.
		13	James baseborne son of Jane Butterfield.
		14	Thomas son of Thomas Denning.
		16	Kathern dau. of Dixi Hickman.
		28	William son of Thomas Brown.
		23	Elinor dau. of Edward Miles.
		28	Margaret dau. of Robert Blithman.
	Sep.	3	Joseph son of John Baylie (embroiderer).
		7	Anne dau. of Timothie Smith.
	Aug.	31	Eunica dau. of Simon Hewes.
	Oct.	10	John son of Brakhouse Miller.
		28	Tho. son of Tho. Faukenbrech.
	Nov.	2	Mary dau. of John Keele.
		6	Christopher Millward.
		10	Mary dau. of Sr Robt. Pye.
		24	Elyzabeth Crosse, Infans.

Parish registers can be an invaluable source for demographic studies of a place. From them you can identify, for example, periods of high mortality perhaps resulting from a famine or plague. They should be treated with caution, however – the ones for Richmond are notoriously incomplete having been compiled by generations of incompetent churchwardens.

churchwardens' accounts, vestry minute books, and records of the overseers of the poor which can be very useful in piecing together the history of a district. These records are best described in W.E. Tate, *The Parish Chest* (Phillimore, 1983), a copy of which should be in your local library.

Many parish boundaries are of great age, in some cases reflecting Anglo-Saxon estate borders. They appear on Ordnance Survey maps, although it may be easier to use the county maps showing parishes published by the Institute of Heraldic and Genealogical Studies, Northgate, Canterbury CT1 1BA. These maps have been collected together in Cecil R. Humphrey-Smith, *Phillimore Atlas and Index of Parish Registers* (Phillimore, 1995), copies of which can be found in local studies libraries and archives.

PHOTOGRAPHS

Local studies libraries, in particular, are likely to have collections of photographs, particularly of old buildings, going back over a century or more. Often they are catalogued by street, so it should be fairly easy to find the place you want. A number of record offices, such as the Hackney Archives Department, are beginning to scan their photographic collections on to computers; so searching (once you have mastered the program) can be done in a matter of seconds.

This topic is discussed in more detail in George Oliver, *Photographs and Local History* (Batsford, 1989). Also worth looking out for is Robert Pels, *Looking at Old Photographs* (Federation of Family History Societies, 1998).

PLACE-NAMES

Place and field names are an interesting study in themselves, as they are often of great antiquity, so may tell you something about the original Anglo-Saxon settlers or the use made of the land they farmed. Much work has been done by the English Place-Names Society, so it is worth looking to see whether there is a volume for your area. A good introduction to the subject can be found in the *Oxford Companion to Local and Family History*, while the best book is Margaret Gelling, *Signposts to the Past: Place-Names and the History of England* (Phillimore, 1997).

POOR LAW

The poor law imposed the obligation of caring for the poor upon local authorities.

An Act of 1603 said that this should be the parish. Overseers of the poor were appointed to provide assistance – usually helping the elderly or the infirm who could not work – and to collect a poor rate from richer villagers. The Law of Settlement could return people who had moved and subsequently sought help from their new parish to the parish where they came from.

By the 1820s it was clear that the Old Poor Law, as this system became known, could no longer cope with the turmoil unleashed by the agricultural and industrial revolutions. A royal commission investigated the position and in 1834 recommended a new system (the New Poor Law) which they hoped would solve the problems and reduce the increasing burden being borne by ratepayers. Some 636 poor law unions were established across the country, run by elected boards of guardians, which set up **workhouses** to house the poor. Conditions here were meant to be such as to deter all but the most desperate. In practise many old people continued to receive pensions (out-relief) at home. By the end of the 19th century this way of caring for the poor was seen as being increasingly outmoded. A royal commission investigated the position but when it reported in 1908 it could not agree a solution. Unions were finally abolished in 1929 and their duties taken over by local councils.

There are a large number of books on the poor law, including J.D. Marshall, *The Old Poor Law, 1795-1834* (Economic History Society, 1985), Norman Longmate, *The Workhouse* (Temple Smith, 1974), and M.E. Rose, *The relief of poverty, 1834-1914* (Economic History Society, 1986).

PRIMARY SOURCES (OR MATERIAL)

Primary sources are historical documents, oral history interviews and other unique material.

QUARTER SESSIONS

JPs initially met together four times a year to dispense justice and discuss the administrative needs of the county. There might be several quarter sessions per county, or the magistrates met in different places on a regular basis. Quarter session records are at local record offices, although their survival is patchy. They are described in Jeremy Gibson, *Quarter Session Records for Family Historians* (Federation of Family History Societies, 1995). The Access to Archives project, co-ordinated by the Public Record Office, is making indexes to all these records across the country available on the internet (*www.pro.gov.uk/a2a/*).

RATE BOOKS

From the mid-18th century rates, a tax on house values, were levied by parish and town councils on houses of the well to do. Initially they were to maintain the poor and highways. Details of the rates paid were entered into large books which are now normally kept at local record offices, although only a sample may have been retained. These books will tell you who owned the property, the name of the tenant if it was rented out, and how much was paid. From that can be built up who lived in a certain house over many decades, supplementing information given in street and trade directories. A word of warning: it can be difficult to identify individual properties in the rate books as the rate collector often entered details following his round rather than street by street. It is also possible to get a rough idea when a street was built, although for the 19th and 20th centuries local government records, such as Vestry minute books, may be a better source.

Further information about these records is given in Ida Darlington, 'Rate Books' in L.M. Munby, *Short Guide to Records: First Series – Guides 1-24* (Historical Association, 1994).

RECTO

The right hand page of a book or document.

SALE CATALOGUES AND AUCTIONEERS RECORDS

Newspapers have always contained advertisements from people wanting to sell or let property, which may give you details about an individual building and certainly give you an idea of its worth.

Sale particulars can often be found at local record offices or local studies libraries. They may tell you how much a property was sold for, any land which was attached to it, the names of the vendor and possibly the purchaser. They are, for example, one way of identifying owners or tenants of public houses. These records are often indexed by property so they should be relatively easy to use.

SECONDARY SOURCES (OR MATERIAL)

Secondary sources are books, newspapers etc in which an event is seen through the eyes of another person, usually an historian, writer or journalist.

TITHES

They resulted from the biblical injunction to give one-tenth of the produce of land to the work of God. Farmers were supposed to give a tithe of their earnings to support the local priest, although how this worked varied from parish to parish. As a result of the rise of nonconformity during the 18th century and the lethargic state of much of the Anglican church this increasingly caused great offence and the Tithe Commutation Act, 1836 converted tithes into rent-charge payments. Tithes finally came to an end as late as 1996 under a Tithe Act of 1936, which extinguished remaining tithes over a sixty-year period. A set of tithe maps and accompanying documentation is at the PRO, while other copies are preserved at local record offices.

The records are particularly useful for checking landownership, field boundaries and field names.

VERSO

The left hand page of an open book or document.

VESTRY

Originally the room in the chancel of a church where meetings were held. By the 17th century the term 'Vestry' was coming to describe the parish council, especially in the larger parishes.

VILLAGES

Historians have identified two types of village: 'close' where the majority of houses were owned by one or two landlords, and 'open' where property was owned by the villagers. Open villages tend to straggle as residents originally built houses on any spare piece of land, whereas close villages are more likely to have an ordered appearance.

John West, *Village Records* (Phillimore, 1997) describes sources which you might use in writing the history of a village. Another, now rather dated book, along the same lines is R.B. Pugh, *How to Write a Parish History* (Allen and Unwin, 1954), although it contains some interesting ideas.

WILLS AND INVENTORIES

Wills exist from the 15th century, although until relatively recently few people made a will. Before 1858 wills were proved in a variety of ecclesiastical courts, of which the most important was the Prerogative Court of Canterbury (PCC) whose records are now at the **Public Record Office**. The records of minor courts are generally at local record offices, although wills proved in the Prerogative Court of York are with the Borthwick Institute, Peasholm Green, York YO1 2PW (*www.york.ac.uk/inst/bihr/*). A national system was established in 1858 and wills since then can be consulted at the Principal Probate Registry, First Avenue House, 42-49 High Holborn, London WC21V 6NP.

Of particular interest to local historians are the inventories of property which often accompany wills between about 1670 and 1783. They itemise possessions room by room, and so give an insight into how a building was furnished and the wealth of the deceased. There is a card index – arranged by name not place – to inventories accompanying PCC wills at the PRO. Local record offices may have similar indexes for inventories they hold.

WORKHOUSES

Workhouses were institutions built to house the poor in conditions that would deter all but the most desperate from seeking help. The first workhouses date from the end of the seventeenth century, but the majority were built during the first half of the nineteenth century. Most houses have been demolished but some remain as hospital buildings and, ironically, as luxury blocks of flats. There are several museums, of which the National Trust property at Southwell, Nottinghamshire will undoubtedly be the most impressive when it opens at Easter 2002.

Appendix II
USEFUL ADDRESSES

•••••

Listed below are addresses and other details for the national repositories to be found in the British Isles.

British Library
96 Euston Rd, London NW1 2DB
Tel: 020 7412 7000
Website: *www.bl.uk*
The British Library is Britain's national library. As a result it is a major resource for local history, although it is primarily a research library. To get access you will need to apply for a reader's ticket and demonstrate why you need to use the library's collections, although access restrictions for non-academic users have been significantly liberalised in recent years. The library catalogue is available on-line, which as it includes the vast majority of books published in the British Isles is therefore a useful resource in itself especially if you are checking what books were published about your area or subject of interest.

British Library Newspaper Library
Colindale, London NW9 5HE
Tel: 020 7412 7353
Website: *www.bl.uk*
The British Library Newspaper Library, which is almost opposite Colindale underground station, houses the UK's largest and most comprehensive collection of newspapers and magazines. You will need a reader's ticket, although main BL passes are also valid. A catalogue to its holdings is available on the website.

Family Records Centre
1 Myddleton St, London EC1R 1UW
Tel: 020 8392 5300
Website: *www.pro.gov.uk/frc/*
As the name suggests the vast majority of visitors to the Centre are family historians, although there are records here of interest to local historians, particularly a complete set of census returns for England and Wales between 1841 and 1891, and copies of wills proved in the Prerogative Court of Canterbury before 1858.

House of Lords Record Office (sometimes called the Parliamentary Archives)
House of Lords, London SW1A 0PW
Tel: 020 7219 3074
Website: *http://www.parliament.the-stationery-office.co.uk/pa/palrchiv.htm*
The Record Office holds the archives of Parliament and also has the papers of a number of prominent politicians. They have the original texts of private and public (ie government) bills and acts of Parliament, together with petitions and minutes of committee meetings on such topics as railways, canals, turnpikes, and enclosure, as parliamentary approval had to be sought before these projects could go ahead. These records are described more fully in Maurice Bond, *The Records of Parliament: A Guide for Genealogists and Local Historians* (Phillimore, 1964).

National Library of Wales
Aberystwyth, Ceredigion, Wales SY23 3BU
Tel: 01970 632800
Website: *www.llgc.org.uk*
The National Library is the Welsh equivalent of the British Library, with considerable resources for the study of Welsh local history. There is an on-line catalogue.

National Monuments Records Centre
Kemble Drive, Swindon SN2 2GZ
Tel: 01793 414600
Website: *www.rchme.gov.uk/nmr.html*
The National Monuments Records Centre is the public archive of the Royal Commission on the Historical Monuments of England. It holds over 12 million items including old and new photographs, maps,

reports and surveys of buildings around England as well as complete coverage of the country in aerial photographs. Many of the photographs can now be searched on-line.

National Register of Archives
Quality House, Quality Court, Chancery Lane, London WC2A 1HP
Tel: 020 7242 1198
Web site: *www.hmc.gov.uk*
The National Register of Archives consists of copies of listings of collections supplied by local record offices in England and Wales. Its indexes can be searched on-line. The Register is part of the Royal Commission on Historical Manuscripts (HMC) which co-ordinates the work of local archives. They also have catalogues for many records held by local record offices in their welcoming reading room.

Public Record Office
Ruskin Ave, Kew, Richmond, Surrey TW9 4DU
Tel: 020 8392 5200
Website: *www.pro.gov.uk*
The Public Record Office (PRO) is the national archive of the United Kingdom and England and Wales. It has records on almost every aspect of English society going back to the Domesday Book of 1086. There are particularly fine collections of maps and photographs. Its catalogue is on-line, and you can also download leaflets about the records from the website. The Office is preparing a reader's guide on sources for local history.

Society of Genealogists
14 Charterhouse Buildings, Goswell Road, London EC1M 7BA
Tel: 020 7251 8799
Website: *www.sog.org.uk*
The Society's Library is a major resource for local historians, with much material that may not easily be found elsewhere. A fee is charged to use the Library for non-members, currently £3 per hour or £12 per day. The Library catalogue is available on-line. An article about resources at the SoG for local historians appeared in issue 78 (March 2000) of *Local History Magazine*.

Appendix III
FURTHER READING

•••••

Listed below are many of the most common general books on local history and how to study it. Where possible the latest edition is given, although it is possible that libraries will have earlier versions of the book. Usually the only change between editions is updating and the inclusion of additional material which the author has subsequently come across. More specialist books are listed in the main body of the text.

Essential books

This is a personal choice of general guides and reference books, which to my mind no local historian should be without.

Robert Blatchford, *The Genealogical Services Directory: Family and Local History Handbook*. The Directory is published annually, by the Directory at 33 Nursery Rd, York YO 26 6NN (*www.genealogical.co.uk*). It largely comprises of thousands of useful addresses, including lists of most British local history societies and archives, together with numerous articles about local and family history.

David Hey, *The Oxford Companion to Local and Family History* (Oxford University Press, 1996). As the title suggests an essential companion to local history. A version was published in paperback as the *Oxford Dictionary of Local and Family History* in 1997.

W.G. Hoskins, *Local History in England* (3rd edition, Longman, 1984). A classic introduction to local history especially from the perspective of buildings and the landscape. Try also his *Making of the English Landscape* (Hodder and Stoughton, 1992).

John Richardson, *The Local Historian's Encyclopedia* (Historical Publications, 1989). A useful, if dated, definition of terms and addresses.

Stephen Friar, *The Local History Companion* (Sutton Publishing 2001) has been recently reissued and updated.

Philip Riden, *Local History: A Handbook for Beginners* (2nd edition, Merton Priory Press, 1998). As the name suggests it offers a simple introduction to many of the basic sources. Despite the title it is rather academic in approach.

W.B. Stephens, *Sources for English Local History* (Cambridge University Press, 1981). The most comprehensive guide to sources for local history, although it is time for a new edition. If it isn't in Stephens – it doesn't exist!

K.M. Thompson (ed), *Short Guides to Records* (2 vols, 1994, 1997, Historical Association). Two collections of concise introductions to many of the records likely to be used by local historians.

The four volumes of the textbook produced for the Open University course 'Studying Family and Community History' by the Cambridge University in 1994 are also very useful and are worth looking out for. Details of the individual volumes are:

Ruth Finnegan and Michael Drake, *From Family Tree to Family History* (Vol 1)

W.T.R. Price, *From Family History to Community History* (Vol 2)

John Golby (ed), *Communities and Families* (vol 3)

Ruth Finnegan and Michael Drake (eds), *Sources and Methods: a Handbook* (Vol 4)

OTHER BOOKS WHICH MIGHT BE HELPFUL

Deirdre Beddoe, *Discovering Women's History: A Practical Guide to the Sources of Women's History, 1800-1945* (Longman, 1998) – an essential guide if you want to study the seriously under-researched area of women's lives at a local level.

David Iredale, *Enjoying Archives* (David and Charles, 1973) – rather dated, but still an interesting look at the research you can carry out using local archival material.

David Iredale and John Barrett, *Discovering Local History* (Shire, 1999) – particularly useful for the medieval and earlier periods.

Evelyn Lord, *Investigating the Twentieth Century: Sources for Local Historians* (Tempus, 1999) – an essential companion for more recent research.

Stephen Porter, *Exploring Urban History: Sources for Local Historians* (Batsford, 1990) – very useful for the history of towns.

Philip Riden, *Record Sources for Local History* (Batsford, 1987). An essential, if slightly dated, guide to records of use to local historians at the Public Record Office: especially useful for medieval and early modern records.

Kate Tiller, *English Local History: An Introduction* (Sutton Publishing, 2001) – rather academic, but again particularly useful for the period before 1750.

FRESH APPROACHES TO LOCAL HISTORY

There are a number of books which take an unusual approach or cover unusual subjects. It may be worth looking at these if you are seeking inspiration!

Donald Brown, *Somerset v Hitler: Secret Operations in the Mendips 1939-1945* (Countryside Books, 1999) – this is a fascinating account of an aspect of the Second World War, a subject which even today is clouded in secrecy.

Dave Haslam, *Manchester England: The Story of the Pop Cult City* (Fourth Estate, 1999) – a unique study which attempts to merge local history with pop history in a survey of popular music in the city from the 1840s onwards.

Michael A. Williams, *Researching Local History: The Human Journey* (Longman, 1996) – one man's explorations, although how he goes about it will raise an eyebrow or two.

Your local bookshop will be able to order any book in print. They may let you browse their copy of *British Books in Print* to check details. If you have access to the internet, you can search the comprehensive database of books held by *Amazon.co.uk* to see whether they have the book you want.

MAGAZINES AND JOURNALS

There are two national journals, *The Local Historian* and *Local History Magazine*. The former appears four times a year and is published by the British Association for Local History. Subscribers to *The Local Historian* also receive *Local History News*, which contains news and reviews from across the country. *The Local Historian* is rather more academic than the newsier *Local History Magazine*. This is published roughly every two months. One of the great strengths of the *Magazine* is its comprehensive reviews of most newly published books on local history, so it is easy to keep up to date with current publications.

Annual membership of the British Association for Local History is £19 a year. For details contact the Association, PO Box 1576, Salisbury, SP2 8SY (*www.balh.co.uk*). A year's subscription to *Local History Magazine* is £17.60, and should be sent to 3 Devonshire Parade, Lenton, Nottingham NG7 2DS (*www.local-history.co.uk*).

It is also worth looking at genealogical magazines, particularly *Family Tree Magazine* or *Family History Monthly*, which often publish articles of interest to local historians. They are usually sold in larger newsagents.

Almost every local history society publishes a journal and possibly other publications as well. The local studies library or record office should have copies of such material published in their areas, or at least be able to direct you towards it.

SECOND-HAND BOOK SELLERS

There are several second-hand book dealers who specialise in local history. They include the Castle Bookshop, The Old Rectory, Llandysill, Powys SY15 6LQ (*www.archaeologybooks.co.uk*) and Chapel Books, Chapel Cottage, Llanishen, Chepstow NP16 6QT.

WEBSITES

The local historian is not as well served on the internet as is the family historian. Many genealogical websites, however, contain considerable elements of local history. The largest British family history website, for example, at *www.genuki.org.uk* contains much of interest. Both the BALH and the *Local History Magazine* websites have links to useful sites. A number of local history societies and local museums have a presence on the web.

The easiest thing may be to type the place or topic you are interested in into a search engine, such as *Altavista, Excite* or *Goggle* and see what it comes up with. Because of the chaotic nature of the internet it may take considerable patience before you find anything of use.

Useful websites are also listed in the appropriate place in the main body of the text.

LEARNING MORE

Many local adult education centres and Workers' Educational Association (WEA) branches organise local history courses of one kind or another. They are certainly worth joining, as they are a very good way to learn more about the subject and to meet fellow enthusiasts. Your local library should have details of all of these courses. If you already teach local history, it is well worth joining the Association of Local History Tutors c/o East House, Rokemarsh, Wallingford OX10 6JB.

University continuing education departments often run courses and seminars on local history. Although some classes are designed for beginners, most are more suitable for people who already have a basic knowledge of the subject. One of the most enterprising is Oxford University's Department of Continuing Education, 1 Wellington Square, Oxford OX1 2JA who run a large number of courses every year, including one over the internet. Again local libraries should be able to advise you about such classes being held in your area. *Local History Magazine* occasionally publishes surveys of available courses. Their website *www.local-history.co.uk* also lists a number of courses, but it is far from complete.

Another way to meet fellow enthusiasts is by joining your local history society. Almost all societies organise monthly lectures. Many also produce a regular journal containing articles from members, which is a good way to publish your own research. Family history societies, too, often have speakers on local history, although of course here the slant tends towards genealogy. Societies also publish booklets or books on aspects of local history, and they are generally always looking for authors, which is another good way to see your work in print – although don't expect to receive any payment. Your local library should be able to tell you about societies in your area, and their meetings are often publicised in the local press. Many are also listed in the annual *Genealogical Services Directory: Family and Local History Handbook*. The Handbook also lists many national special interest societies, which are well-worth joining if you've got a particular interest in, say, brewing, bricks or Turkish baths.

Appendix IV
VICTORIA COUNTY
HISTORY VOLUMES

Bedfordshire	4 vols	Complete
Berkshire	5 vols	Complete
Buckinghamshire	4 vols	Complete
Cambridgeshire and Isle of Ely	10 planned; 9 published	1 volume in preparation
Cheshire	3 published	2 volume (s) in preparation
Cornwall	2 vols	
Cumberland	2 vols	
Derbyshire	2 vols	
Devon	1 vol	
Dorset	2 vols	
Durham	3 vols published	1 volume, on Darlington, in preparation. Some material is being put on-line – see the websites *www.englandpast.net* and *www.durhampast,net*
Essex	24 vols planned; 11 published	2 volumes in preparation
Gloucestershire	20 vols planned; 8 published	2 volumes in preparation
Hampshire and Isle of Wight	6 vols	Complete
Herefordshire	1 vol	
Hertfordshire	7 vols	Complete
Huntingdonshire	4 vols	Complete
Kent	3 vols	
Lancashire	8 vols	Complete
Leicestershire	5 vols	
Lincolnshire	5 vols	
London	1 vol	

Middlesex	20 vols planned; 11 published	3 volumes in preparation
Norfolk	2 vols	
Northamptonshire	6 planned; 4 published	2 vols in preparation
Northumberland	Not started	
Nottinghamshire	2 vols	
Oxfordshire	19 vols planned; 13 published	2 volumes in preparation
Rutland	3 vols	Complete
Shropshire	18 vols planned; 7 published	3 volumes in preparation
Somerset	22 vols planned; 7 published	3 volumes in preparation
Staffordshire	20 vols planned; 11 published	1 volume in preparation
Suffolk	2 vols	
Surrey	4 vols	Complete
Sussex	17 vols planned; 10 published	1 volume in preparation
Warwickshire	8 vols	Complete
Westmorland	Not started	
Wiltshire	21 vols planned; 17 published	1 volume in preparation
Worcestershire	4 vols	Complete
Yorkshire: general	4 vols	Complete
Yorkshire: East Riding	10 vols planned; 6 published	2 volumes in preparation
Yorkshire: North Riding	2 vols	Complete
Yorkshire: West Riding	Not started	
Yorkshire: York	1 vol	Complete

For more information about the Victoria History of the Counties of England, please contact the Institute for Historical Research, Senate House, Malet St, London WC1E 7HU (*www.englandpast.net*).

INDEX

•••••

See also topics listed in alphabetical order in Appendix I: Glossary.

111